To Gerald

from Paddy Boy
6/12/86

voyage

The First

GALWAY HOOKER to AMERICA

1986

Paddy Barry

Gill and Macmillan

Published in Ireland by
Gill and Macmillan Ltd
Goldenbridge
Dublin 8
with associated companies in
Auckland, Dallas, Delhi, Hong Kong,
Johannesburg, Lagos, London, Manzini,
Melbourne, Nairobi, New York, Singapore,
Tokyo, Washington
© Paddy Barry, 1986
7171 1441 4
Print origination by Wellset Ltd, Dublin
Printed by Brough, Cox & Dunn Ltd, Belfast

All photos in the book, unless otherwise
acknowledged, are by Kevin Cronin.

To our wives
Mary, Suzanne, Jane, Catherine, Mags,
Máire and Bríd

Thanks to
P.J. Carroll
who funded the return of *Saint Patrick* to Ireland

CONTENTS

Prologue

'Paddy! Watch your head!' Kevin shouted at me, as the boom of the 'Leath Bád' *Saint John* swung right in over us and they sailed close up. Before we knew what was happening they had heaved three bags of turf onto our deck. With shouts of 'Good Luck' the two old boats swept apart again. We were sailing to America, and Mick Hunt, *Saint John*'s skipper, was giving us a going-away present. Minutes earlier Frank McCarthy's 'Gleoiteog' had sailed by and tossed us a bundle of towels. 'Good luck, lads', he said. 'You might need these'. Conn McCann from the 'Bád Mór' *Connacht* had thrown us a ball of marlin twine — Sean had to make one of his best catches to hold that!

Our boat, the old Galway Hooker *Saint Patrick* was tied alongside the Coal Harbour in Dun Laoghaire. The crowd was growing, and a dozen boats expectantly milled about. Brief hugs and promises to be careful and the lines were cast off. The spars creaked as the red sails went up, first the big mainsail, then the flying jib. Horns hooted, our children, wives and friends waved, the odd tear formed. This wouldn't do at all.

'Come on, lads! Get those fenders in, get those warps coiled and stowed', I said, superfluously, as they had already begun to tidy up.

As we passed through Dalkey sound and rounded south for Wicklow Head the boats seeing us off turned back. It was 5 July 1985, and we were alone and on our way at last.

1

Preparation and Departure

'WHO'D GO on a jaunt like that?' I said to my wife Mary, putting to one side the invitation from New York to bring a Galway Hooker over to the Statue of Liberty for the Fourth of July, 1986. Mary said I should talk to the lads about it. I met Joe Kenny a couple of nights later, and his enthusiasm knew no bounds. His only sailing experience of any consequence had been a three-week sail of under 1,000 miles to Brittany and back that summer in excellent conditions.

The following week-end Fred Rochford declared himself as being a definite starter. Wasn't life rolling on and we were well due a tonic of a few months away from it all. I remained unconvinced. Fred had done even less sailing than Joe. The Hooker was in good order, perhaps, for her age but was very old and not a suitable choice for long-distance voyaging.

But a few weeks later, when Kevin Cronin threw his hat into the ring, I knew, for the first time, that this thing could be made to work. Kevin was reliable: he had sailed with us to France and Spain and round Ireland over the years and was aware of what would be involved. Equally importantly, the three wives gave their blessing (Joe has many friends, but no wife). Sean Mullan declared out initially, even though he was an obvious starter. A good friend from way back, he had sailed in the Hooker more or less wherever she had been in the last ten years. After a few weeks listening to the chat from the sidelines no-one was very

2

surprised that he opted in, but his availability was unclear for the long haul in 1986.

We were now sufficiently crewed up. We organised a meeting, as opposed to the distinctly informal talk and joke sessions that had taken place up to now, in the Punch Bowl. Here, Joe and Fred met Danny Sheehy for the first time. He knew Sean, Kevin and myself since we had all sailed to Spain a few years earlier, and would be joining us in the Canary Islands.

The agenda for that first meeting, held in January 1985, covered the plans and the problems. We reviewed the invitation. Lincoln Paine, of Opsail, had written from New York inviting us to go there, and we had since met him in Dublin. Opsail were organising the Tall Ships Parade of Sail. He seemed like a straight fellow and gave the impression that in a quiet capable way he got things done. Would they cover our costs? His crowd wouldn't be paying anything themselves, but hopefully would help persuade others to do so.

Which way would we go? Ireland to New York by the direct route is 3,000 miles. but that route is dead to windward against the prevailing westerly winds and into the Gulf Stream which flows at about a half knot in the wrong direction. The old sailing ships rarely took this route. A second possibility was the Azores route, about 4,000 miles going by way of the Azores Islands to the south of the westerlies and the Gulf Stream. This is sometimes used by yachts going westward but is very chancy; lack of wind is a problem, due to the permanent large high pressure system bringing fine calm weather to that part of the ocean.

The third option was the Southern route, some 5,500 miles, going down past the Canary Islands into the tropics and across the ocean, turning right (or North) before getting to the West Indies and going up past Bermuda into the East Coast of the USA. Winds and currents are favourable all the way past Biscay. There is also a fourth way, the Northern route, with reasonable winds, but it has cold North Atlantic weather early on giving way to fogs and calms off the grand banks of Newfoundland. This interested us not at all.

3

Departure from Dublin, 5 July 1985

Paddy Barry, skipper and author, who has owned Saint Patrick since 1973.

We chose the Southern route.

The weather dictated that we should leave Ireland between April and August to avoid equinoctial gales in Biscay. The trade winds blow pretty well year-round, once sufficiently south, but the hurricane season runs from June to November on the western Atlantic. We all had job constraints, another factor to be considered. Three of us were employees and three self-employed, but no-one was going to feed our families for us for three months or so while we were away. We decided to sail 1,700 miles to the Canary Islands in July of 1985, moor the boat there and in early May of 1986 leave the Canaries, getting in to the US East Coast before the hurricane season and in time for the Fourth of July celebration.

Our costs would amount to about £20,000. The biggest single item would be getting the Hooker back from the States to Ireland. I wanted not to *have* to sail it back, i.e. to have the wherewithal to ship it back if necessary so that there would be no question of it not coming home. Shipping would cost about £6,000, and there would be our fares to and from the Canaries and the States.

We set about finding the necessary funds, stores and gear. In best PR fashion we got out a semi-glossy brochure, and circulated it. By the time we left in July 1985, we had got mostly what we had expected: plenty of *bon voyage* wishes, generous help with stores and such-like, and no cash of any consequence — but we had high hopes from that traditional Irish standby, money from America. And Gill & Macmillan had asked us to write a book. This was not of much immediate financial use, but it opened up possibilities.

We were now well on our way, Ireland behind us and the Bay of Biscay before us.

———

The tide in the Irish Sea turns to run south one hour before high water in Dublin, and generally vessels set sail 'on the tide'. We hadn't, so the current would be against us until two in the

5

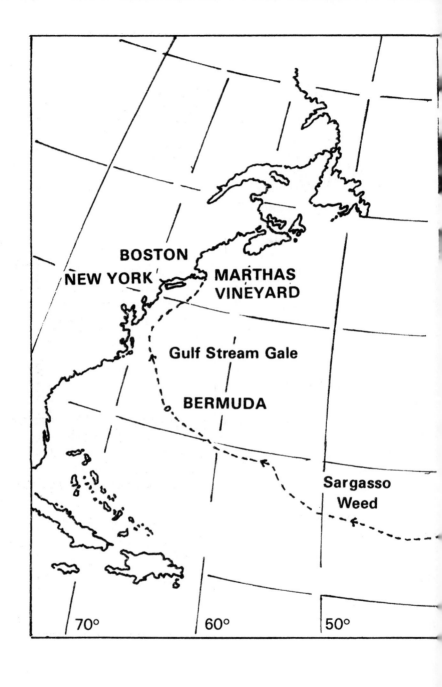

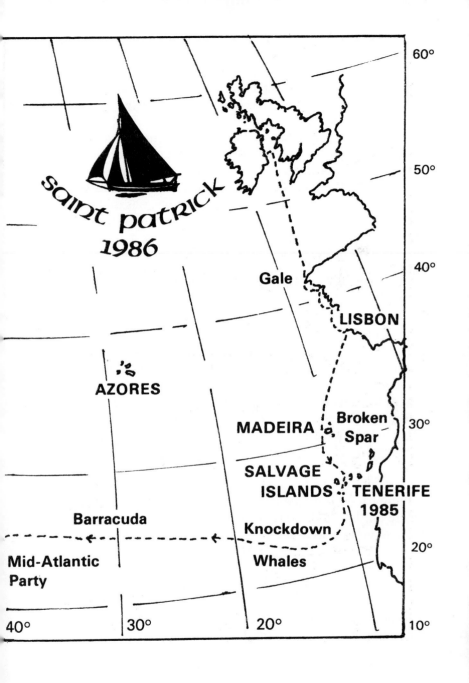

morning. The Met. Office was giving moderate force four westerly winds for Friday and Saturday.

In the event the breeze was very slack. We felt it was unbecoming to be drifting around Killiney Bay with the tide pushing us back whence we came, so the sails came down and the engine went on. We went over our 'man overboard' drill, and who would grab what if we had to take to the liferaft. Sean announced that he would take the food. Lots of ribald comments were passed, as our chef is partial to exotic cheeses, mueslis and the like. He was exhorted to bring food which *everybody* could eat. Fred, strong and reliable, was told that he would be unwelcome in the liferaft unless he had fresh water, at least one five gallon jerrycan and preferably a second (for watering the drinks!) Kevin was to bring fishing gear; he had an impressive array of hooks, lines and lures. I would bring the EPIRB distress beacon and such charts and navigation gear as could be stuffed in a bag: Joe would bring medical supplies.

Sean and myself sat down to work out a system of watches. We wanted to have two men on at any stage, to combine experience with the lack of it and to mix the temperaments if possible. The cook could be absolved from watchkeeping, leaving the four others to share the running of the ship: this makes for terrific meals, but four hours on, four hours off, is not much fun. We like to have two people on, at night at any rate, as it is much more sociable. Most yachts now have self-steering, so that one person is enough to look after a boat, but a Galway Hooker is not a yacht. We went back to a system successfully used a few years before, when there were five of us coming back from Spain. Arrange the names in a circle. Anywhere on this circle start with two, four hours later the next two, go on and so it goes.

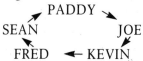

This gave every second off-watch as eight hours, which is not bad. The names were arranged so that Fred and Joe were never together. Fred had plenty of experience working on water and fishfarming in Clare, but not with sailing, and Joe's maritime experience centred around the high diving board. Paddy (myself) was going to navigate. This can be demanding when land is anyway close, particularly at night or in poor visibility. On many boats the navigator would not stand a watch. We could not afford this luxury; we would all stand watches and in rotation also take a day at the cooking.

Off Bray Head the Walker distance log was streamed. Joe, who had done a cruise with us last year, explained to Fred about the logs. One log is written up daily, to keep notes, and the other is a device to measure the distance run through the water. (Wouldn't you think that with all the different salty names there are for things in boats they wouldn't have to use the same word for two entirely different affairs?) The distance log is a rotating propeller towed on a line.

Shortly afterwards the wind came up from the west and we again raised the mainsail and the jib, without hoisting the third sail, called the foresail. The foresail is always the last up, and the first to be taken down if the wind rises. This has to do with the balance of the boat, but it is also the easiest sail to run up or down. As darkness fell Wicklow Head lighthouse started to flash on our bow. There were black squally clouds about, so in anticipation we reduced the area of the mainsail by putting in reefs. This little job takes three men about fifteen minutes in good conditions, i.e. if done in good time, before the wind and sea have already blown up. Kevin and Sean, who had both covered thousands of miles in *Saint Patrick*, went through the reefing routine with Fred and Joe. As it would be a very frequent job it was as well to get the hang of it as soon as possible.

First, we had to drop the foresail to get it out of the way, and heave hard on one jibsheet to pull the jib over to the windward side. The helmsman then eases the mainsheet. If you have three men available, one hauls hard on the topping lift to take the weight of the boom. The other two lower the throat halyard and peak halyard to let the top of the mainsail down about six feet. One man ties a short lashing through a cringle (or eyelet) in the

9

luff or front of the sail to tie down about five feet of it to the front of the boom. All three then work out along the boom tying in the reefing lines to gather in the bottom five feet of the sail. The helmsman pulls in the boom with the mainsheet, without letting the wind fill it, if he can. The outer end of the sail is then lashed down to the boom through another eyelet in the back of the sail. This is the trickiest part, as the action takes place about three feet behind the stern of the boat. Haul up the sail again, peak and throat halyards, heavy work on a bouncing boat. Ease the topping lift, let go the weather jib-sheet and sail away.

'Got it?'

'Sure', lied Joe unconvincingly. Fred rolled his eyes towards heaven.

About eleven that night Kevin and Joe were on watch. A grand pot of steaming stew, made up at home, was landed on the cabin table and we had our first meal. It couldn't have been better and it augured well. Even Kevin, who had his bowl up on deck at the tiller, declared it a winner. The tide was still running up the Irish Sea against us, but by tomorrow we would be away from the cares of tides and watching for shores and sandbanks.

In the year 1909 Pat and Joe Casey bent their backs to lay the keel of the *Saint Patrick*. These two brothers, of a highly regarded boat-building family on Mweenish Island, took two years in the building because they were building her for themselves and in no hurry. The family owned a shop in Mweenish and the boat was to act as a supply vessel to the shop. When the boat was being repaired in the mid-1970s I found the joints so tight that I asked Colm Casey, did they caulk as they put in each plank. He told me no. Their flair for shaping a boat and the skill in their hands will not again be seen. It is a great pity that timber eventually rots!

After two years the Caseys sold her to the Conroys of Rosmuc, who operated a busy general store beside the small stone pier at Garrivan. They were also travel agents, with, it is said, the biggest business in Ireland at one stage — all outward bound on single tickets to America. They would organise the passport, visa and tickets for intending emigrants.

To and fro from Rosmuc to Galway worked the *Saint Patrick* with the imports and exports of this small community. In the summer of 1912 she carried Padraig Pearse, Thomas McDonagh and Joseph Mary Plunkett out to the Aran Islands where they were attempting to organise the Irish Volunteers, with mediocre success it is said. Until about 1970 it was possible to sail a boat through the tidal passageway between Lettermore and the mainland, known as Bealadangan. A fixed bridge now closes this access. Once through Bealadangan on the way eastwards to Galway the boat would travel down Greatman's Bay past Tír an Fhia (Land of the Deer), Maumeen, Collaheige, Carraroe on the hill behind and out into the broad swell of the Atlantic. With a westerly wind behind her she would pass Cashla Bay, Indreabhán, Spiddal and Barna before hauling up at Galway Docks.

Good days and bad, times were changing. The roads into Connemara were being built and improved, and the primacy of the sea as the link with Galway was no more. No new Hookers had been built for many years, and those that remained re-treated to the only trade left to them. *Saint Patrick* was sold to Carraroe, where Micilín MacDonagh worked her with turf to Aran for the next ten years. Aran has no trees and no fuel. For firing, these Islands depended entirely on turf, cut in Connemara in spring, dried in the air and carried out during the summer in Hookers.

In the late 1960s even the turf trade to Aran died: bottled gas saw to that. *Saint Patrick* was sold out of Connemara to a group of enthusiasts in Galway City about 1963, who worked to convert her to a yacht. The sails were reduced in size and a petrol paraffin engine was installed. She was decked and given accommodation. Unfortunately, the engine proved unreliable and the sails inadequate and she was sold to Jim O'Meara in Goleen, West Cork. Jim, for all that he liked her, found her size

11

and condition too much of a handful and after some years at Goleen she passed in September, 1973 into my hands. Never have I experienced so penetrating an investigation into my credentials and intentions as Jim put me through before closing the deal.

All 1974 we sailed and bailed the boat, with more bailing than sailing. At season's end the vague plans for some repairs were urgently brought forward. The steel props and railway sleepers providing jury support for the mast were removed and the good ship landed into my Dublin backyard. There she stood for five years while old stuff was sledged and cut out and a forest of larch and oak consumed in a substantial rebuild. A diesel engine and tan terylene sails were installed to make her move.

Afloat in pristine splendour in 1979 we went around to the traditional regattas in Connemara. Insufficient canvas slowed us, and the Fastnet gale found us anchored in Brandon Bay, Kerry on passage home. Our anchors held, but the three of us were swamped in the dinghy while going ashore about 10 p.m. in the gathering darkness and rising gale. Luckily we were life-jacketed, and made shore; the dinghy was wrecked.

The following year saw us round Ireland under new bigger sails, taking in the Connemara Regattas more successfully this time. In 1981, feeling that our running-in period was over, we sailed the Bay of Biscay to Northern Spain, returning by way of Brittany and Cornwall.

In 1982 we went back to Connemara, again rounding Ireland. The return passage proved hard going; we had to run for shelter from gales on two of the three week-ends involved. The *Saint Patrick* featured on an Irish postage stamp that year. 1983 saw us back in Brittany sailing in company with the *Connacht* which was built about 1830 and is the oldest Hooker afloat.

While one was never likely to grow soft on the *Saint Patrick*, the scene below decks had now become almost comfortable. Five pipecots are tucked under the side decks. These are of canvas, eyeletted and roped to tubular steel frames. They are

Kevin Cronin, an accountant, has been to Brittany and Spain on Saint Patrick.

Sean Mullan, a career guidance counsellor and an excellent shipboard cook.

surprisingly comfortable and dry out easily after getting wet from either bilge water slopping up from below or deck leaks from above.

The Cabin Bunk is the easiest to get into and out of. Just walk over, bend down under the side deck and in you go. It is in the centre of the boat, more or less, so is subject to the minimum of pitching, and is dry, but because it is in the cabin there is always noise nearby and because it is handy, general junk tends to get dumped on it.

The Port Quarter Bunk is dry, and fairly easy to get into, although some agility is an advantage. It is only a couple of feet from the engine; while it may be claimed that the steady throb of a seventy-horse-power diesel has a soporific effect, those who know would suggest that it is not conducive to a restful off-watch sleep.

The Port Forward Bunk is a beauty in harbour. It has the bookshelf, a reading light, headroom to sit up in, and you are most unlikely to be disturbed. It is dark, which makes it easy to sleep by day. It is dry. It may be a little short for some but, lying diagonally, that's all right.

The 'Skipper's Bunk' has one great merit. Once you are in you are tucked out of the way in a cul-de-sac and there is an excellent prospect of getting some sleep. Of particular benefit is the adjacent pot-bellied stove, which makes this bunk a real home from home. To lie there on a typical misty Irish day and feel the warm glow and smell the turf is living indeed. The bunk is somewhat awkward to get into, but when tucked into the hollow of its gently curvaceous bosom, life can feel worthwhile.

The Hatch bunk would be at the opposite end of any scale. It is so wet that people who know put their oilskins *on* when going into this one. Swinging by the hands from overhead, the legs are poked in first and the corpus is vibrated horizontally until all is inside. The steps, fifteen inches from your ear, convey the gentle sound of hob-nailed boots clattering up and down the steps. The hatch above the steps admits not only fresh air, but a goodly proportion of any rain or spray which is going. The cooker, with its kettles, pots and pans, is at the other side of a

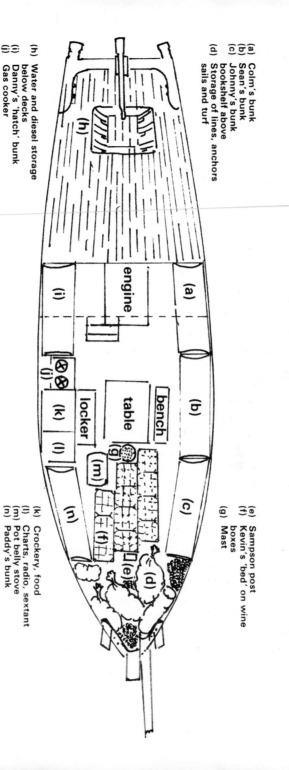

(a) Colm's bunk
(b) Sean's bunk
(c) Johnny's bunk
   bookshelf above
(d) Storage of lines, anchors
   sails and turf

(e) Sampson post
(f) Kevin's 'bed' on wine
   boxes
(g) Mast

(h) Water and diesel storage
   below decks
(i) Danny's 'hatch' bunk
(j) Gas cooker

(k) Crockery, food
(l) Charts, radio, sextant
(m) Pot belly stove
(n) Paddy's bunk

thin plywood bulkhead. The hand pump is also within convenient reach and earshot; the pump discharge is through the hull just over this bunk. It enjoys the same intimate relationship with the engine as its opposite number across the way.

The Coachroof is that part of the deck raised up so as to give extra headroom below. It had been held down by screws and nails; to these we added a dozen through bolts fixing it solidly to resist any sea sweeping over her deck. The deck itself was cleaned off and given a continuous covering of Thermaweld, a bitumen sheet material, heated one side by blow torch and stuck down. A new sampson post was put in, and the cockpit was halved in size to reduce the volume of sea water which would weigh into her if seas came aboard. Some planks, frames, half of the transom and the capping rail were replaced. A cooker with an oven was installed. The engine exhaust was rearranged to stop water running back up into the engine and a trim tab was put on the back edge of the rudder. For years we had sailed unconcerned with a four-man emergency life raft for use if our main transport sank. Now, in preparation for our new voyage, we got hold of a more appropriate size of liferaft. The sails and rigging were unchanged, as were the spars, except for replacement of the two oak jaws to the gaff. These had broken some years ago and had been bound up temporarily up to now. A depth sounder and VHF radio for short range communications had been put in after the Fastnet gale of 1979. The boat has no guardrails to stop one falling overboard but at sea we rig a heavy line from stem to cockpit and hook our safety harnesses to this. Navigation lights are electric, and there are two hand pumps and an engine-driven pump.

Having introduced the boat, it is time to do the same for the crew. Kevin, an accountant, is entrepreneurial, active in community affairs, sporty, and married with four kids (the older ones might object to the description) and has a quiet way. Joe, however, could never be accused of keeping his wit quiet. He was a useful rugby player, as well as a high diver. When we were rearing children he was in Australia, 'tearing minerals out of the bowels of the earth'. Joe is an insurance broker now. He hasn't done much sailing but is a good man to have on your side.

Sean Mullan's character is complex; those of us who have known him for years still find he has a fresh slant on things. He is married, with four boys. Sean went through UCD Engineering with Kafkaesque paperbacks in his pocket, and now teaches in Dun Laoghaire. He played rugby, has done a couple of marathons and acts with the Dalkey Players. Himself and myself, together, started sailing twenty years ago.

Fred Rochford is one of nature's gentlemen. Born in Tubbercurry, he is married and at the time of sailing had one baby girl. Fred is strong, careful and reliable; when you want something done right, Fred's the man.

As for myself, Paddy, a civil engineer, I like water, music and things Irish; like Kevin, Joe and Sean I have done a marathon. I am married with one boy and three girls.

CHAPTER TWO

Journey to Madeira

AN HOUR after midnight the wind was falling and a quarter hour later the engine went on and was still on at two in the morning when Joe and myself came on to find the wind up. The engine was put off. The lights from the town of Arklow were well in sight at this stage. All that night we had some sailing, some motoring, as the wind came and went. There was a chill in the air, but without any sharpness in it.

The course now led outside the Wexford sandbanks; indeed at five we came much too close to the Blackwater bank ahead. Breaking water could quite plainly be seen and an abrupt turn to deeper water was necessary. Years ago I heard that an annual game of cricket is played on this bank! The full run of the tide was now helping us on our way. By eight, Tuskar rock with its big lighthouse was abeam as we passed between it and Carnsore Point.

The first twelve hours were an ideal settling-in, with no stress or strain, and by mid-day we were sailing again with a light but steady breeze from slightly ahead. About that time of day the ship began to hum. The short-wave radio had quite decipherable conversation and we were all up and about. The Cherbourg-Rosslare ferry passed us about a mile off and the BBC forecast gave north-west force four. This was very encouraging. There was also a gale warning force six to eight for Finisterre, but that was a long way ahead of us. At two in the

18

afternoon the last watch had clocked 14½ miles, certainly no big deal but very comfortable and including a hearty breakfast to boot.

During the afternoon the wind freshened. We were forced to steer slightly to the east of our course. The day stayed sunny but never really warmed. A wood-pigeon appeared and tried to land on the boom end. The bird seemed surprised that it kept moving about and made several attempts at finding his feet, without success. It must have been exhausted, because it shortly dropped into the sea about twenty yards behind us. We couldn't see him rise as we sailed on. We consoled ourselves with a salad lunch. With the larder bursting with food, fresh, tinned and dried, the menu could be lengthy indeed.

That evening I took a sunsight. Unfortunately, either the results were poor or we were sailing in a very crooked direction. We soldiered on, preferring to trust in our compass at this early stage until we had more practice with the astro-navigation. A sunsight at any one time does not give a position but only a line. You could be anywhere on that line, but by combining it with a line obtained some hours earlier, when the sun was in a different position, the intersection of the two lines gives the ship's position. In reasonable conditions on previous passages I could nearly always get within five miles or so of the actual location, using a £20 plastic sextant, so I did expect somewhat more accurate results using our borrowed brassbound Kelvin Hughes instrument. Fred drily remarked, 'Maybe it's the workman blaming his tools'.

Day one closed with a good dinner cooked by Sean, washed down with best supermarket red from a square box. 'No more boxes for us soon', said Kevin. The sun had gone down. Piano music played on the cassette. All seemed well with the world as we moved in the right direction with just enough breeze to send us gently along. High pressure seemed to have settled in, and we were moving on its eastern side as it carried us clockwise to the south. The stars rose. The night was so lovely that no one was inclined to go to the bunks. The pungent aroma of Bewley's coffee filled the air. My God, but this made up for an awful lot

19

Joe Kenny who could produce meals in conditions in which no takers could be found to eat them.

Fred Rochford, one of nature's gentlemen.

of wet and miserable times that we had spent on this Hooker!

At six in the morning on the second day, Fred spotted a 'sooty shearwater'. Is there such an animal at all? For years Sean had dazzled us with detailed identification of fauna, on land and on sea; until Fred came along there was no contradicting him. But Fred knew at least as much as Sean in this area and he had brought a book along with him, *Birds of Europe*. Somehow, Sean's identifications were now a little less forthcoming.

A ship overhauled us and continued on the same line. This seemed to indicate that our course was OK, assuming they were also bound for Finisterre. The Scillies passed just below the horizon; they are very keen to be called by their correct name, which is the 'Isles of Scilly,' *not* the 'Scilly Isles'. Our RDF (Radio Direction Finder) had not picked up the Tuskar as we passed, and it now failed to pick up the Scilly signal. So much for electronics.

We changed charts onto the big 'English Channel to the Straits of Gibraltar' one. That had a nice deep-sea flavour to it. We had used it a few years earlier when going to Santander in Spain, but would now be going well out to seaward of those pencilled lines.

Suddenly, dolphins! Three or four, about six feet long, cavorted about. There was a rush for cameras, but as quickly as they came they were gone.

The log reads:

Two in the morning. Distance run, 240 miles. Watch, 18.7 miles. The moon is up to the east and the world is at peace. The wind has been blowing from the north-east since the sails went up again yesterday. We are standing well out to sea from the usual route to Brittany ... The Irish Met. office gave us a five-day read before we left, which is pretty well coming to pass, a little ahead of time. So who's complaining? Please God, it will last. Certainly the prospects of an easy Biscay crossing never looked better.

All bowels have now moved, except for one, who claims lack of initiative on his part, with a possible effort come daylight.

21

Never has there been such a dry boat below, due to a combination of the deck-sealing last winter and the good weather... The hull is taking very little water; a few minutes pumping a day is hardly necessary. The new propellor shaft-brake keeps the shaft from turning. This is probably the reason for less water intake, and certainly makes for a quieter ship.

Kevin greased the gaff jaws yesterday. He climbed the mast using the lacing as steps. Before then there had been quite a creaking, and presumably wear, where these oak pieces rub the mast. I never heard of greasing the jaws in Connemara, or come to that in any books or magazine articles either. It is such an easy thing to do, with so much effect. The predominant sound now, down below, is that of water rushing past the hull... The shrouds were tightened during the day and this has stopped the rattle of the shackles. The cooker creaks a little as it swings on its gimbals – now there's a little job for tomorrow.

During job time yesterday we filled five jerrycans of diesel into the tank to top it up. We have a total of thirteen with us, I think. Our first water jerrycan is nearly empty. That's OK. We have plenty of soft drinks. The diet thus far has had a predominance of vacuum-packed ham. As the weather gets warmer it will be interesting to see if we can get through it before it goes off.

8 a.m. I made a shortwave contact with Peter White, our 'Saint Patrick Base'. We'll have to change the radio schedule so I can get some sleep.

Fred was cook of the day but there was a diminished appetite for his wares as there were now white horses on the sea all the time. The wind had backed slightly towards north-north east making steering more difficult. We dropped the foresail. Joe, who has a cast-iron stomach, was regaling us with tales of his previous holidays in the Canaries and promising us a high time when we got there. The engine, which was being run in neutral to charge the batteries, stuttered and stopped. Trouble-shooting the diesel engine as the boat pitched and rolled was a real sickener. There was no fuel getting through one of the

22

three filters; the fuel line was rearranged to by-pass this filter and everything was then humming. It sounds easy when you say it fast. It was in fact a miserable hour of alternate retching into the bilge and working with diesel-soaked spanners and rags.

9 July. Midnight. The night shift writes again!
Powering along on a virtual dead run. Two reefs in the main-sail and working jib on the bowsprit. The work on the helm is very heavy and concentration has to be 100%. If one sails more than five degrees above the course she tends to round up into the wind. The full blast of weather and waves then hit you. It is a dark night with the moon not yet up. There are stars but there seems to be a slight haze as they are not very bright.

We had a hard time sorting out the throat halyard just before dark. I had actually seen this fouled earlier in the day. The rope had wound itself round the outside of the block in such a way that it would not run. This was dangerous, as it meant we could not reduce sail area to fix it. Kevin and Joe hauled me aloft in the bosun chair, bringing the foresail halyard up with me. The mast swayed wild arcs through the air and it was work to hold on with hands and legs. I put my safety harness around the mast and attached the foresail halyard to the throat. The lads hauled on that and made fast, taking the weight off the throat halyard. I was then able to prise off the fouled line.

The reception on the BBC had been weakening. The music they play just before the midnight forecast is very soothing, called 'Sailing By'. It reflects very well the mood of the BBC in Britain, but very rarely the mood of our sailing. Something which conveys a little hardship would have been more appropriate.

At 1 a.m. I got into my oilskins and harness to go up on the helm. At 2 a.m. Joe took over. We did 21½ miles that watch and before hitting the sack we had a ball of malt. Very nice!

At ten in the morning Fred and Sean, going off, announced a new watch record, 22 miles. However Joe declared it not allowable because it was 'wind assisted'! Our noon shot of the sun showed a 16-mile gain on the distance log reading. This indicated a southerly current of that amount in the last twenty-four hours. Our latest plot gave a distance to Cabo Finisterre of 175 miles. We altered our course from 194 degrees to 189 degrees.

That evening we took down the big jib and replaced it with the two smaller working headsails. Just before dark we had to drop one of those as the wind was rising further. We were now picking up Spanish on the VHF. I was off until 6 a.m., an eight-hour break, so to add to it treated myself to a cigar, courtesy of Fred, and a whiskey. Earlier that evening we had had a radio schedule with Peter. He didn't come on, but a pal of his from Belgium who called himself 'Alternative Saint Patrick Base' did. These fellows are never stuck for jargon.

Our plan was to stay outside the shipping lanes off Cabo Villano and Finisterre and keep going for Bayonna 70 miles on. However, if we got a decent forecast and could make Camarinas behind Villano by sunset we thought we might go in there. It got dark that night about half-past nine, contrasting with half-past ten only a few days earlier in Dublin.

10 July, Wednesday. In a weak moment of elation Joe had promised to buy a round for the watch who would clock up the highest distance. Just when it looked as if the skipper and Sean had to be stood, along came Kevin and Joe, who have just put in 12½ miles in their first two hours. Who'll be drinking now? Keep tuned for report at the end of watch.

They did 22½ miles. The following watch did 23½. By 6 a.m. the seas were bigger, there was a half moon in a clear sky and the sun was yet to come over the horizon. As each wave passed beneath the boat she would surf before the wave ran on. When the daylight came the sea was a mass of white waves on a long ocean swell.

At 8.30 Joe recorded: 'Dolphins in abundance were sighted again'. He added (before anyone else did), 'Also missed again by Joe, who had no film in the camera.'

A pigeon tried to land on the boom.

Bad weather in Biscay.

We were flying. The boat had to be kept in line: if she rounded at all broaching might follow. Conditions below were deteriorating and on deck things were not good. Urinating in the bucket at the bottom of the cabin steps and tipping out onto the deck above became of necessity socially acceptable: it was a damn sight safer than performing on deck.

My trousers have a wet backside where a wave came over the stern and ran up my oilskins while I was at the helm. We are holding the course. When the sun comes abeam in about an hour's time I will try to get a sunsight to get an east-west position line. Pumped dry with the hand pump. Washed up. Running the engine for the first time in a couple of days to charge the battery.

At the close of myself and Joe's watch we had done 26 miles, an average of $6\frac{1}{2}$ knots. The sunsight had given us a position which put us on the coastal Spanish chart. Despite our wet condition we felt in control and I decided to close the coast. We hardened sheets and altered course to the east, steering 164 degrees. For the rest of the day the log was virtually bare of comment. 'V. poor conditions', was all it said.

The wind rose, the sea rose. The foam blew off the wave tops in streaks. We got the mainsail and jib down and with engine on and steadying foresail headed shorewards, land still not in sight. Three o'clock came, four o'clock, still nothing in sight. I was worried and trying not to show it. Then land appeared over our heads, only about a half mile away, it seemed. The seas eased. We met a French yacht sailing downwind under her headsail. We went towards a bay, which we thought to be Camarinas, but it wasn't. We altered course, rounding Villano, and dropped our anchor in the quiet water off the pier of Camarinas by evening.

Ashore, we enquired for somewhere to eat and dry out, and were directed up the village. The bar/restaurant didn't look much, with its terrazzo floor and TV, but Romano fed us well on hake (we think) and wine from the barrel.

About two in the morning Fred made a phone call home, and got the rest of us into trouble for not doing the same. Considering it was our first night ashore we retired in reasonably good shape, and conked flat out.

By ten next morning we were under sail, going south, with no particular objective in mind. Yesterday's big wind was gone. We drifted and fished. After a while we decided to go into a sandy beach which lay invitingly inshore. An uneventful afternoon was spent in slothful idleness until about five, when we set off under motor for the village of Muros about twelve miles on.

We passed Cape Finisterre, one of Europe's great headlands, according to the book. It did not appear that awesome to us, perhaps because, being used to the west coast of Ireland, we are not easily impressed by scuttery little headlands. The book also said that it was the most westerly point in Europe. We thought that the Blaskets were in Europe!

Our information sources were threefold. The Charts, showing in great detail the coastal features, the rocks, shallows, headlands and bays, were generally surveyed by navy men in between various wars in the mid-nineteenth century. They were done to such a high standard that corrections are rarely necessary. Allied with those are the Admiralty Sailing Directions, also called Pilots. These give the tidal streams and the climate and describe the coast, mile by mile, rock by rock. They were written by steady prudent men, which is reflected in the sombre prose style. The growth of pleasure boating has given rise to 'yachting directions' for the more popular areas. These have mainly been written in recent years, with smaller boats in mind. They have photographs and detailed harbour sketches, often describe the facilities of the places and are invaluable in picking a place to moor.

We went into Muros. The fishing fleet was in. After some shouted conversation, in Sean's best Spanish, we lay into a berth at the end of the harbour wall. Quite a little crowd gathered to look us over and talk to us. Muros is a substantial lively town, with a mile-long busy street curving around the harbour. Our first stop was the quaintest shop you have ever seen. We are not strangers to licensed premises where tin buckets, sacks of meal, soap-powder and the like are equally available but this place could only be described as 'more so'. There wasn't a thing in the place looking less than about two hundred years old, including the woman behind the counter. She gave us wine from the vat for a few pesetas. We went again and again and only she hadn't anything to eat we might never have left it.

As we lay to our bunks, the town clock chimed the hours over the still harbour. Tomorrow we were off to Bayonna.

The alarm clock went off, after only a few minutes, it seemed, but it was half five. A dense fog enveloped everything. The harbour had emptied of fishing boats while we slept. Carefully we double-checked the course and motored out.

About mid-day, the sun broke through. The Isla Cies showed ahead, a group of islands fronting the Ria De Vigo. By late afternoon a good breeze gave us a fine sail the eight miles or so to Bayonna. We passed too close for comfort over the shallow rocks off Las Estellas and were relieved to see the figures on the depth sounder rise as we cleared the shoal and got into the main Bayonna approach. It was a big town, a major yachting centre. With 'élan', we hoped, we carried sail through the moored fleet and brought up off the end of the main finger pontoon. Here boats were berthed in the mediterranean way, stern-to the pontoon, so we motored ahead opposite a vacant spot, dropped our anchor and went hard astern into place. At least, that is what we did after our second attempt.

Here was activity. We paid the 800 peseta (£5) charge in the major yacht club which has a bar, restaurant, showers, boatmen, shipwrights, fuel and all the accessories, and we used the showers and the bar.

Our next stop would be in Portugal. By dawn we were well down the coast but, unfortunately, without any stir of a breeze, so it was engine all the way. The land lay a mile or two to the east

28

of us, a mountainous backdrop of brown, although the guide books call this the green part of Portugal. The coast here is quite shallow for a couple of miles offshore and we had to take a few sharp right-hand turns as the depth sounder showed shoal water when we crept carelessly in to get a better look at places. There was a big number of open boats, about 26-foot long, at sea. They each had three or four men who were very friendly, always a shout and a wave if we were anyway close at all. As far as we could make out they were longlining. At first we made great efforts to keep away from the buoys; in summer in Ireland, the waters within five miles of the coast can be a cat's-cradle of salmon nets and lobster pots with long polypropylene lines waiting to foul the propellor of the unwary, and often the wary too. Here the lines from the buoys went straight up and down and you could go right past them.

We passed the Duoro River, gateway to Oporto, at noon. This had been a possible stopping place, but it was somewhat early in the day. The coast now changed from low cliffs to sandy beach, miles and miles of it. The next possibility was described in our directions as 'a small town, with a harbour for which improvements were planned'. As we continued we saw what we took to be oil tanks or towers. Gradually it became clear that they were apartment blocks, dozens of them, and the beach was covered with people. Could this be the same Povoa De Varzim? Sure enough, there was the harbour entrance. Harbour improvements! The old harbour lay in a corner of this huge complex. The place was chock-a-block with fishing boats.

Hardly had we tied up but we noticed, no, that is not the word, winced at the music coming over a very effective loud-speaker system from the town. Joe and Kevin took shots of some friendly boys. And Carlos came. Carlos Alberta Ferreira, as he later wrote down for us, is a teacher, aged about thirty, who had left Mozambique after the Portuguese were thrown out. We were to meet many from Angola and Mozambique, back in the home country for the same reason. Carlos spoke good English and was very friendly and full of information. The town itself had become the Blackpool of north Portugal, but

Carlos brought us to an upmarket 'English' place called 'Brooks'. We got a kick out of the sound of cicadas coming from behind the pictures of English countryside hunting scenes.

Back on our floating home, about midnight, we had a bit of a barney about our programme. We had been pushing it a bit, with all the midnight flits. We had originally agreed that it is good to move at night, when there wouldn't be a lot doing, and get ashore for late afternoon and evening. For half-an-hour there was a very 'frank exchange of views'. The air was cleared, and off to sea we went, ever southwards. The night was calm and clear, without wind. We stood single one-and-a-half-hour watches. Joe noted in the log: 'Mildest night so far. Listened to the Portuguese radio. Not surprised this country is better known for its sailors than its music.'

The morning dawned dull, and around nine it actually started to *rain*. This lasted only for five minutes. We were still motoring for lack of wind. Our only immediate fixture was to meet Johnny Walsh, who was joining us for the next leg, in Lisbon on Thursday afternoon, about a hundred and fifty miles away. This was Sunday. There was a forecast of good sailing wind from tomorrow, so we decided not to go any further than Figuera De Foz.

The day developed into a scorcher and a north wind came up to give perfect sailing past Cabo Mondego and up the river right into the basin of Figuera. Wandering around that afternoon, we saw traditional folk-dancing in the park, followed by an army band. Kevin wandered surreptitiously, trying for 'character' shots of the local population. Joe appeared with new white shoes, Fred a sunhat, I bought shoes and sandals.

An hour after midnight we put to sea under sail. The wind, which had risen yesterday afternoon, was still up. The Portuguese Trades, which are supposed to blow consistently from the north in summer, appeared to have arrived at last. By eight in the morning sail area was reduced and shortly afterwards the mainsail was fully reefed in. We passed inside the Berlenga Islands; tee-shirts were necessary to protect the shoulders from

30

sunburn. By late afternoon the headland of Cabo Raso at the mouth of the Tagus river was in sight. The wind had risen further. This must be the 'nortada', a strengthening of the wind, which translates into 'hard north'. With short white waves all about we turned the corner eastwards. The Hooker lay well over with her gunwale kissing the water. At least the sea was now fairly flat. We rounded into the bay of Cascais, intending to anchor there. There is no quay. However the wind was such now that getting ashore would have been dangerous, if it was possible at all. So we carried on up the mighty Tagus where by dark we were berthed in the hospitable (meaning they didn't charge us) marina of Club Naval De Lisboa. A full gale had risen in the last few hours and we were glad to be out of it.

For three days we toured the city, visiting the monuments, maritime museum, old quarter, the lot. The Tower of Belem was only four hundred yards down the river from us; this was built as a highly decorated fortress and was the last sight the old Portuguese saw as they started their world voyages. It is the symbol of Portugal. Beside us was the new memorial to the 'discoverers', a tall structure in a plaza on the riverside. Mosaiced on the plaza is a huge map of the world with the Portuguese voyages shown. On the outside of the monument are ranged the 'Desperadoes', as we called them. It shows the head man up front, followed by his retinue of soldiers, clerics and sailors looking out from the bow of a ship with a billowing sail overhead. It is easy to criticise them now for the savage treatment they meted out to their conquered unfortunates, but they were savage times. What is in no doubt is their courage, and the level of science they brought to their navigation was far ahead of its time. Lisbon prospered on foot of it and the many broad streets, magnificent squares and monuments are testimony to this wealth. Today Portugal is a poor country, but in the sixteenth century Lisbon was the wealthiest city in Europe.

Wednesday night was the boys' big night out. All five of us loaded into a taxi and headed off for a place we had heard was good — Harry's Bar. As we drove up the narrow street the taxi-driver was giving us funny looks. Joe, sitting beside him,

31

chatted on about us being sailor men, in from the sea, thirsty for love, lovely Portuguese girls, dancing, when suddenly the driver laughed and said 'Dancing, si, alles hombres, gay bar!!' A quick change of plan followed: we went instead to a 'fado' place, a down-market 'Jury's cabaret'.

The next day Johnny Walsh joined us, as arranged, by plane from Dublin. Since Danny was not on this leg of the voyage we had room for another hand. Johnny was more of a mountain-climber than a sailor; however, on previous local passages on the *Patrick* he had been good company and 'sound in wind and limb'. His attitude to life is robust, favouring the head-on app-roach to joys and problems both. He is a solicitor, and hadn't yet found the time to get married.

We got the boat ready for sea and had a subdued evening. Tomorrow we would be bound for the islands of Madeira, five hundred miles to the south-west.

The 'Nortada' had us scared by now. Each afternoon saw a full-fledged gale from the north, and several yachts bound south-ward were still around. The Lisbon Met. Office said it would be less windy far out from the land. How far? We couldn't find out. We left at the dawning of Thursday, streaming the log off the Tower of Belem and getting under sail off Fort Buggio, the sand-bank fortress which guards the harbour.

Course was set 260°, to the north of the direct line, in anti-cipation of heaving-to the 'nortada' and the southerly current. We reckoned that we had until about two in the afternoon to be well clear of the land before the wind would blow up. By seven the sky was clouding over. At eight the foresail was dropped as the breeze picked up. At 9 a.m., 'really moving at 6 knots'. At 10 a.m.: 'We have sailed approximately 15 degrees south of our course for the last hour and a half'. At 12 noon the boat was on course, and at 1 p.m. 'sea lumpy but the boat is not hard to handle'. The distance log was giving us between five and six miles every hour. At two in the afternoon the sky was inclined to clear. We waited for the blast from the 'nortada'.

At four we still hadn't got it, and conditions on board must have been O.K. for writing:

32

We put all the reefs in the mainsail about an hour ago. The sky is fifty per cent cloudy and there are squalls about which hit us about every twenty minutes or so. Our speed has dropped but we are very snug reaching along to a beam wind ... The extra man aboard makes life much easier. It is terrific to be off eight hours at a time. Also in reefing the work was easier, granted we reduced sail in good time. Sailing rigout is oilskins over shorts and tee-shirt, shoes optional. The hatch bunk is uninhabitable due to water. We think it is coming in the scupper. P's bunk has a couple of minor leaks.

Just now the wind has freshened and there is 100% cloud. It is grand to have the reefs already in and not be sailing on the edge, spilling wind from the sail with your gut in a ball. Johnny, Kevin and Sean are lying in the port bunks sleeping/dozing. We should have a good meal tonight. There is fresh meat in stock.

A contented lot we must have been. At 6 p.m. Joe was getting the dinner and Kevin fishing. Domesticity itself. On the short-wave we failed to raise Peter again but by chance came across a maritime network in English. This is an inter-yacht frequency where boats who have licensed Ham operators aboard come on each evening for a half an hour exchange of news and then get weather forecasts for the various areas of the eastern Atlantic. We were unlicensed, so could not talk to them, but they did assure us that our signal was loud and clear and of course they would respond if we had a problem.

The sky cleared during the night and the wind eased but we didn't bother taking out the reefs until dawn. We were now steering 230°. The dawn brought a light drizzle. A couple of fishing boats had been sighted an hour before daybreak. Kevin noted during the morning that he had a 'benign watch with azure winds and a spanking pace'. It's hard to whack that. He also notes his consumption of his first Erin Foods dehydrated 'Little Dinner', which he declared to be excellent. This was no news to Joe who had been downing them, in between times, for weeks.

Johnny Walsh.

Danny Sheehy.

Sometime later that morning the clanger came.

'Sean, where's the milk stored?', said Fred.

'Why, is the litre gone already?'

'What do you mean, the litre?'

Yes indeed. Our quartermaster was not one to throw our money around in overstocking. For six of us on a five-hundred-mile passage he had shipped aboard one litre of milk! He took a while to live that one down, despite his protestations about the plentiful supply of dried milk we had, the careless over-use of the litre, etc. etc.

The watch rota was changed in the afternoon so that sun-sights could be taken on the skipper's own watch without disturbing my beauty sleep. Sights put us somewhat to the west of our course and we altered ten degrees. The big jib went up and the sky cleared with much lazing around the deck for the afternoon. That day the sea became a deep turquoise, or was it royal, blue. We argued about the colour. It was an extraordinary deep hue. Even with the sun occasionally covered with cloud, the colour of the sea did not change. A naval vessel, 'U 26', slowly crossed astern of us. It carried no identifying flag and did not respond to our radio greeting. Fancy that.

The day finished with real coffee, a sure sign of ease and comfort as making this requires more effort than the instant coffee.

The sky is now cloudy throughout. There is a force four breeze off the starboard quarter, lifting only a notch in the squalls, which is less than their dark look would suggest. We are half reefed and could have handled the full sail but this makes for a snug night. Signs on it, all the off watch appear to be asleep. We have now settled into a sea routine. Fortunately or unfortunately, by this time tomorrow we will have broken the back of this passage, with thoughts turning again to shore attractions. The forehatch is fully open and there is a good breeze blowing through the cabin, although the heat below has not been a problem yet. The sounds are pleasant tonight, the clink of the anchor chain up forward, the creak of the locker lid that I am sitting on, the occasional grating of the gaff jaws carrying down the mast. There is the sound of the stern-wave through the main hatch and the gurgling of the sea through the hull.

The wind is from the north-east but the swell is from the north-west. There must be a storm up there sending its waves down to us. Nineteen miles this watch.

The next morning was a grey one with the wind dead astern. A couple of squid, about three inches long, were washed up on deck overnight, and were kept for bait. We were now tacking zig-zag downwind, about ten degrees off the direct course. It is difficult to steer the Hooker directly before the wind in any ocean swell without danger of gybing. Fred noted in the log, 'Visited again by "madeira petrel", who has been with us for a hundred miles or so; not unlike a swallow in appearance and size and in its darting movements. In seas of two to three metres high it has the knack of gliding over the waves, often at a height of mere inches, without getting wet'. That was followed in the log by a monetary analysis; Joe was our banker for shore-going finance. The extra few days in Iberia had sadly depleted the 'tank'. All of us seem to be debtors in pesetas, escudos and iou's. Sean baked curranty bread, which was eagerly demolished, and I did some sewing on the sails. The philosophy of companionship was discussed lethargically. At 3 a.m. Kevin wrote 'The topping lift came off the boom. Retrieved. Secured. An incident at last. Maybe we'll get some normal hooker sailing again'.

The following day, the detailed Madeira Islands charts were produced and studied. Porto Santo was the nearest island.

'What is our ETA Porto Santo?' Three a.m. tomorrow.

'What if we skip it and go on to Funchal?' ETA would be 11 a.m. tomorrow. Through the clouds we snatched a brief morning sunsight and, after plotting it, altered our course to 210 degrees. Fred helmed our four hour stint, chatting away. At about 2 a.m. we dropped anchor within a new harbour just beyond Porto Santo lighthouse.

CHAPTER THREE

Madeira to Tenerife

IN THE MORNING, into the sea before breakfast. The big new harbour was empty, bar a half-dozen small open boats in a corner and floating construction equipment. We moved out of there a mile further down the sandy bay and anchored off a landing jetty. We were planning on pushing on to Funchal by evening, so allowed ourselves only a couple of hours here. Porto Santo has the flavour of a desert island about it. The only greenery is the shrubs around the houses fronting the sandy beach. A daily ferry and small plane flight are the island's link with the outside world. During our short spell a plane was due in and one bus, several taxis and most of the population of the village, with their mopeds and bicycles, were waiting around to meet it. It could have been Kilronan in the Aran Islands, if the tropical surroundings were ignored, or indeed any of thousands of small remote islands around the world where the focus of life is the link with outside.

It was here that Christopher Columbus, as a young sea captain, found his bride, the governor's daughter. It is also said that when the Romans and later the Portuguese first landed on Porto Santo they returned to Europe without being aware of the bigger island of Madeira. This, however, seems unlikely, as on any sort of clear day its outline must be visible.

We were only an hour out of the bay when Madeira formed through the haze. It was predominantly green, dotted with red roofed houses and isolated apartment blocks. An aircraft runway was cut out of the side of a mountain inclining upwards (or downwards, depending on which way you look at it). We saw two planes take off in the hour it was in view. As they left the runway they turned sharply to starboard as they climbed and swerved to avoid the mountain ahead. We presumed it figured on any list of non-favourite airports.

The wind fell to almost nothing, leaving us to drift and then motor into the big Funchal harbour. Until recently Funchal was a major crossroads on the highways of the sea. The liners to and from the colonies used it. Within the main harbour lies an enclosed smaller section for sailing boats. We slowly rounded up outside this, stowed sail and looked within at its crowded scene. Slowly nosing in past an assembly of boats, we eyed a spot, got the impression that it was OK and turned our sixty-foot length in what seemed like a fifty-five foot width. There was some discreet reaching for fenders and boathooks by the watching assembly, who had more than an idly curious interest in the success of our manoeuvre. Realising the futility of a twelve-foot boat hook when faced with a sixteen-foot bowsprit, they took to fervent prayer. We swung round and in, dropped fenders in place and tied up.

For three days we lay in this harbour, a major gathering spot for long-distance sailors. The talk was of trade-wind crossings and distant places, self-steering and solar generators. Some four dozen boats were there, of many nationalities. The general type of boat was different from that one gets used to in northern marinas, where the more visible yachts are of the racing type, single-masted light boats with minimal equipment. Many long-distance cruising boats have two masts so that the sail area is more easily handled by small crew. They tend to be heavier so that they can carry the stores and equipment to remain self-sufficient for long periods. They carry heavier ground tackle, dinghies, spare jerry-cans and self steering.

An impressive singlehander was tied up across the way from us. A Swiss double-ender, she was about forty feet, GRP. On her stern were Aries steering gear and a Danforth anchor, line

Repairs to the broken gaff in Madeira.

Identify yourself! An immature herring gull visited us for half an hour until mutual boredom set in.

and chain, ready to be let go. Also on her stern was a roll of line on a reel, presumably for trailing as a man overboard precaution, or it could have been for fishing. Roaming on deck was an evil looking Doberman: it was most unlikely that that boat would be broken into. Astern of us lay *Germania IV*, a huge yacht, reeking of deutschmarks. There was nothing on it which looked more than a month old. It had on board a couple of 'captain of industry' types, a couple of paid hands and about ten keen clean youths. They spent their time quietly polishing invisible specks from the hull and cleaning stainless steel crockery, enough to kit out a hospital. Each time I passed they seemed to have some different exotic equipment hanging out. It takes all sorts.

The Madeirans have a strong sense of identity and independence. They recognise their dependence on the 'Peninsula', as they call Portugal, but see it as separate from their country. They have strong connections, through emigration, with South America, Venezuela in particular. In public monuments they make a virtue of this. The discovery of Ihla Madeira, the island of woods, is generally credited to De Zarco, a Portuguese. Some people we spoke to were a little incredulous when we explained that this was the rediscovery, Saint Brendan from Kerry having called there, amongst other places, a thousand years earlier. There is ample literary evidence of this, but as far as I know no physical evidence.

On Thursday morning we left Funchal, bound three hundred miles southward for Tenerife, one of the Canary group. The Salvage Islands, an uninhabited group of rocky islands and reefs, lay midway. Captain Healy of *Asgard II* had warned us of the tidal set in that area. The notorious pirate, Captain Kidd, is reputed to have lost a ship there with two million pounds worth of gold and silver, stolen from the Spaniards, who had in turn brought it from Peru. We timed our departure to be in that area during daylight.

At seven we left with the sky brightening to the east. We streamed the distance log, checked our steering compass against our two hand compasses and made a six-degree adjustment. A swell came in from the north-east but there was no wind so we motored. By ten the shelter of the island was no more and the north-east wind was blowing us on our way. There was one foresail up and half reefs in the mainsail. The log noted: 'Plenty of sail, flying along on a quartering reach. The shaft brake is not completely tight. In the surges the propellor spins'. Three-quarters of an hour later the wind had freshened further, with steep seas breaking white. We prepared to reduce sail area and all hands were roused. Just as we were moving into position to get the mainsail reefed it swung across with an unmerciful gybe. Gear went flying. Joe and myself at the stern were bloody lucky not to have been swept over in the tangle of the mainsheet. The topping lift came off the back of the boom and our gaff was broken in two. 'Drop the sail when I round up', I shouted, through the wind, spray and confusion of lines, to the lads at the foot of the mast. But the sail would not come down. They heaved, hauled, pulled lines separately and together but the top of the mainsail would not budge. We were in trouble.

The jib was taken in while the engine held the boat to weather, and we considered the situation. The twenty-four-foot spar was snapped in two pieces. The seas were rolling the boat about making a bosun-chair inspection, not to mind working up there, dangerous. We could not reach the clew of the sail to cut its lashing and brail the sail to the mast. Ilha Deserta lay upwind to the east about thirteen miles. There, according to the sailing directions, we would find an uninhabited island populated by goats and wild tomatoes. We put back for Madeira.

Slowly and painfully we made ground. By early afternoon our anchor was down in a sheltered cove outside of Funchal. Repairs were straightforward in these easy conditions. The topping lift ring was replaced on the outer end of the boom. I went up the mast in the bosun chair. The lacing on the gaff had caught round the protruding pin of a mast shackle, and in the abnormal gybe this had fouled. A hacksaw cut to the line freed it and both halves of the gaff and the mainsail were then lowered. The sail was taken off the broken spar. We had on board lengths of two-by-one timber for general spare purposes, and with a half dozen of these a splint was put on the fracture. The sail was made up and in a couple of hours all was ready again for sea.

This job could have been done at sea but would have taken a half day or even a full day and would have been hazardous. The sail had suffered a tear and the masthead light had got a belt and was hanging loose. The light was taped up and left there; we did a temporary sew-up on the sail.

Because we wanted to put into the Salvage Islands we postponed our departure until the following morning. This time we had full reefs in from the beginning. Sure enough, by the time we had passed the scene of yesterday's unhappy event the wind was up. Now we were cosily snugged down and moving easily before the seas.

Yesterday has been a reminder of what the sea can do if your guard drops. We had been complacent with our references to the three-hundred-mile 'hop' to Tenerife, 'taking in' the Salvages. Now we are on our way again in good heart, looking forward to a steady passage and getting to Tenerife in three days' time. Items on the boat which need improvement are clothes storage. The netting over the bunks used for storing the clothes sags too much. Rubbish in port is also a nuisance. The gash bucket at the bottom of the hatch steps is unsightly as well as being in the way.

While I was lying on deck, Kevin from the helm made an urgent whisper to get the camera. On the port gunwale a large speckled bird had come to rest, identified from our book of birds as an 'immature lesser-backed gull'. We gave him a feed of bread and stayed for about half-an-hour until mutual boredom set in and he (she?) flew away. The rest of the day passed pleasantly. We could have knocked out some of the reefs but we chose to take it easy; we did not want to get to the Salvage Island area before daylight the next day.

That evening after dark the log was written up.

Going well for little effort. It seems to have got chillier. Maybe it's the effect of a bit of a burn from the earlier sun.

The topping life broke adrift from the boom end about half an hour ago. It has been retrieved but not put back on. As we are under all reefs there is no great urgency about it and will fix it tomorrow.

Later that night Joe wrote, 'Just spent a delightful night, perhaps the most personally memorable so far. Now feeling moved to convey thoughts, a tranquil moonlit semi-tropical night with moon nearing the full to guide our course off the bow and the plough off to starboard.'

As the dawn broke about seven, Fred sighted land on our port bow, Selvagem Grande. We hardened sheets and close hauled for these islands, which are small and not that easy to find. We had the detailed 1938 Portuguese chart and a photostat copy of the page in the *Africa Pilot*, Volume 1, which deals with them. It said that the northern group of islands were volcanic in origin and owned by a company in Madeira, that the big island was bordered by steep or perpendicular cliffs but that there was a possible landing place, weather permitting, on the south west side, 'Enseada das Cagarras'. During the three hours it took to close the island we had ample time to study the chart and directions to pick an approach through the offlying rocks and reefs.

About ten in the morning we hove up outside Cagarras Bay. The shelter looked excellent, but what was that on the shore? Was it a house? Holy cow, it was. Two of them in fact, and some people moving about. And a flag of some sort. Kevin was keen to do some fishing so we drifted for half an hour or so before moving in to anchor. There was great excitement as our fisherman caught one, two and then a third exotic-looking fish, later identified as 'trigger fish'. The anchor was sent down in thirty feet of clear water to a rocky bottom. However it was not holding well, and the rocks on either side were close by, so we went ashore in two separate groups.

Myself, Joe and Johnny went first and were met by a couple of

Is beag a ceap mé to
mbeinn amuigh i lár an
Atlantic agus mé ag
stiur ar bád conraí ag
dul go Meirica.
Colm Dubh Ó Méalóid

Selvagem Grande — the largest of the Salvage Islands, 150 miles
south of Madeira. Captain Kidd is thought to have lost a treasure ship
in these waters.

very friendly Portuguese, with whom we talked in sign language. They walked the island round with us. It is a plateau of some one mile diameter, five hundred feet high There are some signs of former habitation and water ditches, but no houses apart from the two at the landing place. All our information was that it was unlit and uninhabited. This has been incorrect since 1980, when the Portuguese built a solar-powered light and put a keeper on the island. It was remarked that this might have more to do with fishing and mineral prospects than with navigation. Joe stayed ashore with Kevin, Sean and Fred. He met everyone, had the full story and would write it in the log. Verbatim, more or less, here it is.

There are two permanent Portuguese wardens living there. These are game wardens as the island is a preserve. Their duties are to prevent slaughtering of the birds, tend the lighthouse and to defend the island! They live in the house at the landing-place. They are visited twice yearly by ornithologists from the Portuguese government and universities, who observe and ring the birds. The timing of our visit coincided with the hatching season and on that account there was a lot of activity. Some chicks had already been born a few days ago ... The second house overlooking the bay is owned by Mr. Zito. His son, in his forties, said that Zito purchased the culling rights to the island some years ago to prevent the wholesale slaughter which had been taking place for food purposes ... The family come twice yearly and also observe and ring birds, independently of the group in the other house, with whom they don't speak! ... When Mr. Zito's three-year lease expired four years ago he encouraged the World Wildlife Fund to purchase the island. The Portuguese Government would not agree to this and bought it themselves, hence the fellows in the house below.

The fellows in the lower house said that in the old days the Portuguese used to put goats and rabbits to breed on islands for the benefit of shipwrecked mariners. No serious attempt was ever made to colonise this island because of lack of water. Provisions are brought into the island, and Zito and friends get there, courtesy of the Portuguese navy. They supplied a further titbit on the British, on whom there appears to be no love lost. The British have the name wrong. The correct translation of Selvagem is not 'salvage', but 'savage'. We gave them a present of some Bewley's coffee before we left.

While swimming in the bay we saw that the rocky bottom on which the anchor lay had some deep ravines. If the anchor went into one of these and got caught we might never be able to get it up. As it was, the chain was wrapped around some outcrops. To get it up Joe went in the water and with a facemask sighted the chain leading to the bottom. He then directed the boat astern, ahead and so on as we hauled in the chain. This was decidedly uncomfortable in the confines of the bay with the rocks so close. Our hook came aboard once again, we plucked our swimmer from the water and pointed our bowsprit for Tenerife.

———————

Good sailing conditions through the night brought us within sight of Point de Anaga, the northern point of Tenerife, by eight the next morning, Sunday. We hoped to reach Los Cristianos on the south of the island by that evening. Mary Barry, Catherine Rochford and Johnny's girlfriend, Mags Wyer, would be there to meet us.

The sailing directions said that a belt of calms generally extends fifteen miles to leeward of Tenerife, that the sea in these calm areas is frequently rough and irregular and that heavy squalls are experienced which give little warning. Thank you very much! We headed for the windward east side. From Selvagem to Point de Anaga was eighty-two miles as measured on the chart.

All day with a brisk following wind we coasted down Tenerife's east side. First came the large city of Santa Cruz. Low clouds and what looked like smog or mist enveloped the city. We passed south, straining to see Mount Teide, but could see no further than the brown lower slopes. Minor hills rose and fell on the coastal plain sweeping down to a rocky foreshore with occasional coves. Some of these had modern apartment blocks in clusters. Just north of Pointe Montana Roja a beach and pier fronted a busy resort with beach umbrellas, windsurfers and the usual paraphernalia. Round Montana Roja, it really was red, could be seen the airport, one of two on the island. It was very busy, with several planes moving while we passed. We later learned that every day is a busy day there. The British turnaround on Tuesdays, the Scandinavians on Wednesdays, the Irish on Sundays and the Germans all the time.

Our deck and cabin were like a laundry now as shaving gear and shampoo was unearthed to make us smell nice again. Fresh water was applied unstintingly. Fats Domino sang on a cassette. Passing Pointe Salema, a shoal sounding worried us for a few minutes until the depths ran up to double figures again. The lighthouse of Pointe Rasca was rounded. As we came into the bay of Los Cristianos the wind fell. Down sail and we motored towards the harbour entrance to tie up just before dark at an empty part of the quay wall. A small crowd of locals, visitors and European yachtsmen gathered and we chatted to them. Shortly after, our wives arrived. They were delighted that we had made it on the appointed day.

We were going to break the voyage and leave the boat here for the winter until we would come back next May to continue. The plan had been to leave the boat moored in Los Cristianos harbour. To this end we had brought, in addition to our own four anchors and chains, some twenty fathom of inch-and-a-half chain, three-inch wire rope and similarly-sized shackles and a swivel. However we found the holding in the harbour to be poor. The bottom was a rock floor with sandy patches. This would not provide a reliable grip for the anchors.

In the harbour there were a dozen sailing boats. Half of these appeared to be on the move and half had been there for months or, in some cases, years, with their owners living aboard them. Their lives seemed pleasant, but boring. The freedom of the seas was theirs but they appeared cloistered.

47

Anchored outside the lot was a large white schooner with steeply raked masts, carrying the American flag. She was a beauty. *Victoria* was the name carved in gilt letters on her broad transom. We met up with her skipper, Jim Hollywood, and he invited us aboard. What a boat! Seventy-two feet long she was, a copy of the famous *America* that first thrashed the British to win the cup of the same name. But she was thoroughly modern in every aspect of her materials and equipment. She had the lot. The owner's bathroom had a mosaiced jacuzzi, for God's sake! The owner was in the States and Jim had just received orders to bring the boat back. Three of her crew, English lads, all paid hands, came aboard the Hooker for a blast round the bay. It was an eye opener to them and they were delighted. All this work, raising the anchor, pulling sheets, hauling halyards, all without winches, was new to them. They reckoned they had had more exercise in that few hours than in the previous month in *Victoria*. Jim gave us some short wave frequencies that he thought might be useful to us in the Atlantic.

The local boatyard is run by a Fishermen's Co-Op. Their yard has a travel-lift, a most impressive piece of machinery which can lift boats of up to fifty ton out of the water and wheel them off and drop them wherever required in the yard. We got prices from them and after a little ruminating, not much because we hadn't much alternative, arranged for *Saint Patrick* to be lifted out on Friday.

But before that, our last sail. From Los Cristianos to San Sebastian, the capital of Gomera Island, is only twenty-one miles. A mere puddin' for men who have sailed the ocean wide! Or so we thought. This was to be a 'promenade sur mer', a sea picnic for the entertainment of the wives and a trio of German acquaintances, Helmut, an occasional dinghy man, Isabella and Martina, Joe's party from the previous night. Motoring out of the harbour, only an hour and a half after the appointed nine o' clock start, life felt good. There was diesel in the tank, bottles of wine in the bilges and sun warming the deck. The breeze, a force one from ahead, offered no scruple to our consciences as wind sailors. There was no need for distance log or compass with Gomera looming out of the haze. A casual remark about white seagulls in the water ahead went unnoticed. About ten minutes later a cry was heard as the first wave ran several inches of water down the towels spread on the deck, the next wave drenched all of it and the next one ran in the open portlights and hatches. Pandemonium ensued. Oilskin jackets were dug out of storage. Picnic baskets flew. Some people felt sick. A northerly force seven had come out of the blue on our starboard bow, throwing up steep six-foot breaking seas. How could this be? We were in about a thousand fathoms, mid-way between the islands. There was nothing for it but to hang on. Weren't we lucky not to have had sail up! And for an hour and a half we crawled forward, praying against fuel blockages and air locks. The women would not have been reassured or amused by salty phrases involving 'heaving to', 'bare poles', 'short sail', 'running for sea room' and so forth. We eventually swept round into the shelter of the harbour of San Sebastian and tied up alongside the wall beyond the two inter-island ferries.

We lost Mary Barry and one of the German girls to the ferry. For the return journey, all reefs were put in the mainsail and a 'barróg' put in the flying jib, by tying in the top one third or so. Oilskins and safety harnesses were buckled on and we took off like a dose of salts. Helmut had never in his life seen anything like it. We hung on, with rigging and sails bar-taut. And then mid-way between the islands the wind fell as quickly as it had come up earlier. The ferry caught up with us. The ship was tidied and we engined back to Los Cristianos.

The following day *Saint Patrick* was lifted out of the water and put standing in the yard beside some fishing boats up for maintenance. All day we worked, stripping rigging and sails from her, washing the sails in fresh water and scrubbing the bottom. The hull appeared in good order but the extent to which the planking would shrink in the heat was a major question mark. There was little to be done about it except to leave water in the bilges up to the floorboards so that at least the lower planking would stay tight. The guys in the boatyard were very helpful and seemed to know their business. The yard manager arranged to get the tear in the mainsail fixed in Santa Cruz and to get the makings of a new gaff from the pine forests on the north side of Mount Teide. He would also keep the bilges topped up with water.

The next day we worked on the inside. The main thing was to clear all traces of food and to strip all items which might appeal to any local 'magpies'. For one reason or another most of the electronics had to come home anyway. The shortwave radio I needed because I wanted to try and work for a licence to make our use of it legal, or at least less illegal. The Auto-helm wasn't working, neither was the Radio Direction Finder. The rudder-head needed strengthening. The eyelets on a bunk canvas needed renewing. The propellor split pin was manky. The cooker, new and all as it was, needed some gaskets at the burners. Working in the cabin in that yard was bloody hot, I can tell you. And then all was done. We could do no more, only lock the hatches and with feelings of sadness, walk away.

CHAPTER FOUR

Departure from Tenerife

'SIT DOWN and I'll give it to you straight', said Frank Ryan.

It was the following January. The *Saint Patrick* had been five months out of the water and Frank had just returned from a visit to Tenerife. He knew his wooden boats from way back, and was a man whose views commanded respect. 'She's in a most unhappy state, her paint is blistered and flaking, her spars have opened up long shakes and her plank seams have shrunk badly', he said.

'Could you get a knife blade through the seams?' I asked. Frank told me that you could get blade, handle and all through a lot of them. He showed me photographs he had taken and they were not funny. He recommended that I bring out a supply of high-quality silicone joint filler, adding that it was my hide that was involved and that he was worried about the boat going to sea at all.

Of course, I had known there was going to be shrinkage of the timbers in the heat, especially as the boat was out of the water. It was the extent that had been unpredictable. I consulted with Joe Murphy, a master shipwright.

'Tallow is your best man, mix it with soap and sawdust and force it into the seams', he said. 'It will form a temporary seal until the wood swells and the squeezed-out tallow can be wiped off. Whatever you do be careful about caulking her. If you hammer in caulking it will fill the joints with a hard material

51

that will leave very little room for the planks to swell again. You could get bursting of planks and pulling of fastenings. And when the boat does go into the water don't sail her for a while. Remember that the timber will have shrunk away from the nails and that until she tightens up any hard going could shake her to pieces.'

Good God, that's the trouble with knowing too much! So I got hold of a couple of stone of tallow, not so easy these days — it's a product of animal fat, used for making soap and also by plumbers for making leaded joints. Afraid that it might melt in the heat we did tests, but it remained stiff at 90° Fahrenheit.

Danny Sheehy and myself were to go out three weeks ahead to get the boat ready. Danny is from Ballyferriter in Dingle and he had sailed on *Saint Patrick* with us to Spain in 1981. Some years before that he had rowed round Ireland in a *naomhóg*, as the Dingle version of the Currachs are called. He spent ten years teaching woodwork, in Drogheda mostly, before going back home with his wife Maura and two youngsters. He fishes round the Blasket Islands. He says himself that 'I have no song and I have no step'. But can he tell a story!

The money situation was still not good. But a dance in Boston and another one in Dublin, the night before Danny and myself went out, had raised enough to help us keep the show on the road. The Dublin night also ensured that it was two very tired lads that arrived in Los Cristianos on the evening of Saturday, 20 April, 1986.

Early the following morning the two of us set to work on the outside of the hull. And she needed work! Her lovely shape was as ever but her condition was even worse than we expected. From one side to the other, at the seams, you could see right through her. The paint was flaking off, and a right derelict she looked.

After that first day working on the seams with tallow we decided it would not do at all. The stuff was melting in the heat and running out again. And the gaps were too wide. If we put the Hooker in the water all the pumps in Tenerife wouldn't keep her afloat. There was nothing else for it; the ship would have to be caulked. We enquired for a shipwright. However the 'carpentaria' would not be available for a week, until the following Monday. There was plenty for us to be doing in the meantime, even if it was in the wrong sequence. First thing should have been to get the hull into the sea so she could be taking up.

The rigging was got out, the blocks were greased and the running lines set up. We wire-brushed and scraped the loose paint off the hull. Our wire brush lasted only five minutes before the bristles fell out. During the ten months in Tenerife, the wood in the brush had shrunk. Luckily we had arranged that the bilges would be kept filled with water up to the floorboards inside, so the bottom three or four planks had not shrunk.

Although the batteries had been new in Ireland I fully expected that they would be run down after ten months. Not at all. They cracked the engine into life first go. Here was something else working out.

There is nothing inexpensive about the Canary Islands anymore. With the exception of petrol and drink bought in shops, prices are as in Ireland or even higher. We bought a new battery for a car, very decently loaned to us by Donal Skehan from Clontarf. Nine thousand four hundred pesetas it cost us (£45). And the 'carpentaria', when we did get him, was 10,000 pesetas per day. However, Antonio turned out to be worth three times that.

We had been anxious about whether he would turn up or not. He did arrive, but he very nearly didn't start work at all that Monday. He looked at our ship round and round, shaking his head, pointing first to the joints, then to us and speaking rapidly to Carlos, our interpreter.

'Antonio say you must work on the joints, cleaning out and preparing for him. Many days, he come back'.

'Cripes', says we, 'we can't delay any more, we are supposed to be leaving for America in two weeks'. As we were saying this, Danny jumped up on a barrel, hammer and iron in hand, and started cleaning the joint between two planks by punching in the loose old putty. He shouted, 'Hey, is this right?' Antonio

53

showed what he wanted and Danny was away on the job. Me too. Antonio stayed and we were relieved. One caulking iron only he used, for joints wide and narrow. Each was filled to perfection, hammered in not too hard, not too soft. When he wove the string of caulking-cotton it was always the right thickness. We prepared the joints ahead of him and red lead painted and puttied behind him. He seemed surprised that we kept going. 'Mucho Travail' he would say. While we would have to lie on our backs under the hull to work overhead, Antonio seemed to be able to crouch upright, 'like a rat' as Danny said, and make the most awkward places seem accessible. Antonio was some kid, a supreme artist of the shipwright trade, and a decent and friendly man to boot.

I could write a book about the day we went for a timber spar to replace the broken gaff.

When leaving the Hooker in Los Cristianos boatyard arrangements were made that they would organise a new gaff. Once we were gone, 'easiana' had set in and nothing in that line happened. All was now to be set right. A conversation between Antonio, a Spanish boat broker who spoke excellent English and myself concluded that the makings of a spar were to be found in some not too far away place which Antonio knew. Purely a collection job; it could then be shaped, and the fittings from the old gaff attached to it.

The following morning Antonio arrived with power planes and heavy electric drills. Very impressive. Into our borrowed car himself and myself climbed, me driving, and 'arriba', off we went, Antonio waving me on the way. Along we drove, up the Santa Cruz road. About ten miles on, Antonio indicated a filling station. 'Pull in'. I did. He then proceeded to ask me, as far as I could make out, where we were going, 'What!' says I. An interpreter was urgently required, but unfortunately not so easy to find. There was much talk of 'ferretaria' which I understood to mean a metal pole or street light. 'Ah, no', says I, 'esso barco traditionale. Timber bene'. Much shaking of heads. Santa Cruz, the main city in Tenerife, about fifty miles away, began to feature in the conversation. I was worried.

The heat in the Canary Islands opened up the joints. Practically the whole boat had to be recaulked.

Antonio, our master shipwright, cuts an abandoned telephone pole to length. By that evening it had been transported to Los Cristianos and formed into a new spar to replace the broken gaff.

'Comprendez?', Antonio would say to me looking up street lamps and tapping them. Neither of us had a clue what the other was saying or thinking.

'Come on', he said, 'Arriba', and we drove off, leaving the main road and going up and up into the hills, past terraced fields with irrigation channels everywhere, to find ourselves in the old town of La Granadillia. We called to about three houses there, being directed onward each time. Then to an official building of some sort into which Antonio went and a quarter of an hour later emerged. 'No vendre' he said. Off again, occasionally stopping and Antonio talking to people.

At some stage, I don't know when, the quest changed. We were now no longer looking for houses and people but were pulling up in open spaces and looking into dried river beds, behind old sheds, under wrecked lorries. We drove up and came to the small village of Chimiche. In no time we were at it again, looking into backyards. And there we found it, lying among the cactus — a beautiful pole about 27 feet long, a 'palo telephono' which had somehow got left behind when the lines were being put up.

Way below a 'hombre' was hoeing a field. A shouted conversation between Antonio and him brought the 'hombre' up. A quarter of an hour into the discussion the word 'pesetas' came into focus and I was apparently being invited to join in. 'Seven thousand pesetas', our friend said in Spanish. To be sure, I asked him to write it in the dust. He did, and it was.

'Esso hombre sincero', I began, pointing to my well-worn runners and paint-spattered trousers, and with all the cares of the world offered him five thousand. Done at six. Not bad for our new 'amigo' — thirty quid for something which it was most unlikely he had any claim on, other than that he was in the right place at the right time.

We sawed three feet off it and dragged it up to the side of the road. It was a lovely light timber, free of knots, 'finlandia pino' said Antonio. And now the fun began. How were we to get this yoke the 25 to 30 miles down the mountain to Los Cristianos? A fourth fellow joined us. He looked somewhat simple to me,

56

but Antonio seemed to be paying a lot of attention to him. All four of us got in the car and drove off.

We found a fifth 'hombre' who was apparently the man we wanted. He had a hoe over his shoulder and I found it hard to see the benefit of this connection. This fellow disappeared and we waited. Twenty minutes later a sturdy 3-ton truck drove along and stopped. 'Perfect', says I. Much discussion ensued featuring the words 'palo pequeena' from Antonio, and from the truck driver 'quanto meters'? Unsmiling and shaking his head he drove off. 'Holy cow. That truck was perfect, and what else are we going to get up here?' I thought.

The four of us piled once more into the car and I drove, as directed, about a mile. We came back to a warehouse with a bigger truck, praise the Lord, outside and 'Smiley' standing beside it. After very little delay Antonio says he wants eight thousand pesetas to deliver it. I began my routine, 'esso hombre. . .' 'Smiley' was unimpressed and began to walk away. Feeling that I lacked aces, I hastily told Antonio, 'Fine, fine, decent man, 8,000 is fine'.

We cleared the pallets off the big truck and three hours later our stick was in the boatyard. By nightfall our new gaff was made up, ready to go on board. I felt a little like a chicken who had been plucked.

For the following two days Danny and I got stuck into the puttying and painting so our ship would be ready for launching on Saturday. Painting in the warm sun was a pleasure. The paint ran free and dried quickly so two coats could be put on during the same day. Peculiarly, they don't have or use undercoat as I found out when I looked for it. When the final coat of 'peintura negra' went on *Saint Patrick* she was a treat to look at. And we painted a white stripe on the bend.

We settled our account with the boatyard somewhat unhappily, as they claimed to be a month short in the payments received. I knew that all payments had left our Dublin bank but as the yard operates on a 'no cash, no splash' basis we had no alternative but to pay the extra £120 they claimed was missing. With some trepidation we waited for the water to pour through her as she was lowered into the sea. But no flood ingressed. Indeed it was three or four hours before she filled to the floor boards and the water intake reduced after that. Although she needed continual minding for the next couple of days, there was no middle-of-the-night pumping called for.

Now we loaded on stores. First diesel, and twenty-three jerrycans of water. At two days per jerrycan of water, and a thirty-day passage to Bermuda in mind, we would take 50% extra for contingencies. In Tenerife tap water is not generally drunk. I don't think there is a lot the matter with it, just that it doesn't have a very nice taste. Danny and I had been using the tap water for the previous two weeks without ill-effects, so we loaded up with that. Our diesel would take us about 400 of the 3,000 miles to Bermuda if the need arose.

Next day we bought and loaded on the dry and tinned food. A mile outside the town there is a 'Kasur', cash and carry, for supply to restaurants, where goods are sold by the case. A second run was made for our stock of wine; we planned on two bottles per day for thirty days to Bermuda and as much again from there onwards. With reasonable wine priced at about £1 a bottle and the beer in Bermuda reported to be over two dollars a go we felt that the dozen cases of wine was a 'good buy'. We thought about buying a case of 'Irish' at £6 a bottle. But money was tight, so that was scrubbed.

On Friday, 9 May Kevin, Sean, Johnny and Colm arrived with an incredible quantity of baggage. Colm O Méalóid from Rathcairn was joining us. Joe Kenny had had to 'cry off' for business reasons, and Fred Rochford was expecting an addition to his family. Joe and Fred maintained, in jest, that the back of the voyage had been broken in getting to Tenerife. 'There's no challenge left', joked Joe. Johnny was with us again, this time as a 'full member' of the team. Before he left Johnny and Mags got engaged.

After a quick sortie from the airport to the Hooker, it was now 3 a.m. All except Colm and myself made a dash to town for a drink just as the last bar closed. Saturday morning saw a lazy sort-out of bunks and gear. In the draw for bunks Danny had drawn the 'hatch' bunk. But Kevin, drawing number six, had no bunk at all. He settled in on the cases of wine stored on the floor up for'ard. A test sail and run over the safety routine was done in the afternoon — and there was no question of being late for the pub that night. Danny and myself gave the lads the benefit of our acquired in-depth knowledge of the watering spots we had grown to know so well. To tell the truth we were tired of the place and the sooner away the better it suited us.

Sunday, and thoughts of the morrow's departure being imminent, saw a full representation at last Mass in Los Cristianos. Sean stocked up on the fresh provisions, green tomatoes, bananas green on the stalk and so on. Kevin and myself had to go to Santa Cruz for an engine part. The car had to be left to a panel beater for attention. On the mid-afternoon of Monday 12 May a small group on the quayside wished us well as we untied our lines from the shore.

———————

A fresh breeze was blowing across Los Cristianos harbour as we raised the three sails, the mainsail with all reefs in. The forecast was north-easterly force seven. We steered to the south-east to clear the lighthouse and once off the coast began to pick up the true north-east wind. It came in fits and starts as we lay-off on our course to the south of Gomera. We would also have to clear the most westerly of the Canary Islands, Hierro, 75 miles on. We were all fatigued from a combination of late nights and work on the boat. Watches were set; Paddy and Colm, six to ten; Sean and Danny, ten to two; Kevin and Johnny, two to six.

Colm had done only a little sailing on the *Saint Patrick* but being originally from Camus in Connemara he was no stranger to boats and 'bádóirí'. An uncle of his had been lost off a 'Bád Mór'. Colm and I had known each other from occasional Galway Hooker Association socials and races. He lives in the thriving 'gaeltacht' of Rathcairn with his family and he works in Tara Mines. His ability to play the 'box', to sing and to dance a set was well established. How would he work in with our confined group on a small boat? We didn't have too long to wait to find out.

59

Some first night out! Sean and Danny harnessed in the cockpit in wet conditions. A few hours later we had been capsized.

The following day, Johnny running under foresail. The seas are still dirty.

The wind rose as forecast and we took down the foresail. However occasional gusts were much heavier and threatened damage to our bowsprit or to the sail set on it so we took in the jib too and continued, quarter reaching and running. This was difficult sailing but tenable once the ship's head was not let come around. The grey evening felt anything but tropical.

Dark fell about nine and at ten Danny came on deck to take over the tiller. The wind was now whistling through the rigging as we surged along.

'We'll have to take down the sail', said Danny. 'No', said I, 'we'll keep it up and drive on, keep her stern to the seas,' and I left himself and Sean to it.

They had a heck of a time holding her from rounding up. Blasts of wind followed lulls, and occasional seas came on us from the north-west, crossing the general north-east seas and wind. I lay in my bunk trying to shut it out and get to sleep, although I knew from experience that you don't sleep much the first couple of days out.

Suddenly in my dozing I felt and heard an almighty crash which filled the air and blotted out all other noise. There was water everywhere and objects flying all over the cabin. I scrambled out of the bunk opposite to the one I had been lying in. I had fallen across or rather down into it. 'My God, the mast!' I thought and rushed to get the engine on and the big pump started. Coming out the hatch I looked first, to my eternal discredit, at the mast and only then to see if all the lads were still in the cockpit. Johnny and Kevin had been up too. Thanks be to God, they were. Everyone was now on deck harnessed and clipped on. Colm in his bunk had taken a full belt of solid water which poured in the half-open hatch beside him. We could see that the mainsail was torn and the mainsheet and topping lift were in a tangle.

'We'll get the mainsail down then the foresail up', I yelled. 'Colm, will you see if that engine pump is working, if not get the hand pump going straight away'.

It was now three in the morning and any doziness had been washed away. We all realized how vulnerable the boat was,

61

laden with water and the running rigging in a mess.

Sean later described the wave that turned us over as having been like a dark wall from ahead of the starboard beam. It had blotted out the foaming white seas towards which we had been running. There was an instant of quietness, he said, just before it struck. Then water everywhere and the boat lying almost gently, he said, over on her port side, just like a dinghy capsize, except that the sea ran right over boat, sail and mast before she lifted vertical again. Danny more simply said he thought we were finished.

An hour and a half it took us to get the tangle down on deck and lashed. Several times in hopelessness we were tempted to use the knife on the running rigging to resolve the mess but we all knew that the first night of a long voyage was not the time to be chopping up rigging. The foresail was got up and immediately went tight as a drum. Occasionally, whatever way the wind and sea would combine, it would go slack and then fill with a crash that would shake the whole boat. 'My God, how will the caulking and dry timber stand up to this?' I thought. But it seemed that it did. Colm had pumped out the boat and was now keeping the level down with the hand pump, working about ten minutes in twenty. Occasional wave tops still swept the decks but there was little weight in them. Everybody and everything was so thoroughly wet that the further spurts of water coming into the cabin through the now closed hatch made little difference.

Cold comfort it brought when, about seven, daylight came. The top of the mast appeared to be very out of joint. The top metal band, which supports the topping lift and VHF aerial, was lifted off the mast top and hanging crookedly. The mast head light was swaying loose. A lifebuoy, a tarpaulin and the sail cover had been swept over. We knew that the mainsail was torn but didn't know how badly or if any of the eyes had pulled out. The wind was blowing force eight or so. This was more or less as it probably had been but without the sudden blasts which had been there before. And the seas were down, or at least they were coming in a regular pattern and from the same direction as the wind. We forced ourselves to get the kettle boiling to make scalding tea which spilled out of the cups over our hands and oilskins. We pumped the boat dry and handed over to Danny, first up, and Sean.

By 2 p.m. the seas had eased, we were feeling somewhat better, and a more serious matter emerged. The rudder was loose on its mountings. Over the stern we could see the 3-inch thick rudder timbers jerking maybe a 1/4-inch within the metal straps which fix it to the boat. There are three such straps, two of which are under water. Were they better or worse?

We considered whether to put back for Hierra or Gomera. We had no information on the harbour in Hierra and the harbour on the west side of Gomera might well have a roll. This would make work at the masthead almost as awkward as at sea. I felt that all the problems could be dealt with at sea — maybe not immediately but certainly when we were in better shape. Sean thought we were mad to go on and told me so. The others said nothing. I decided to keep going and this was accepted by all. Privately the rudder worried me. What if we couldn't fix it and it got worse?

The sail stitching could be tackled immediately and it was. Sail needles, twine, sailmakers palm and with a rough and ready herringbone stitch I drew the four foot tear together. A more thorough job would have been to sew on a reinforcing patch — that was left until some other time.

By evening we had each managed some bread and ham. Spirits felt marginally better than the low ebb at which they had been for the last twenty-four hours. Johnny cracked a joke and Colm went to work on the rudder. A combination of shrinkage of the oak rudder timber away from its bolts and the huge stresses put on it had caused the loosening. Not only was it moving within its ironwork but the ironwork on the sternpost was also loose. Colm hung over the stern, legs held Blarney-stone-like, and managed to drive in a line of heavy boat nails between the steel straps and the timber to wedge the lot effectively together. Well done, Colm — one problem less. We would get this ship together and sailing right yet.

63

We rigged a bosun's chair and I was hauled aloft. However, because of the wild swinging of the mast, I could only just make out the problem, not to mind the solution, and came down without having got anything done.

Tuesday night was gentle but we made it more so by sailing undercanvassed for a restful night. Wednesday morning brought a positive air with it. To-day we would fix the mast-head, as soon as a good breakfast would put body and soul together.

Reach was a fundamental problem at the mast-top. In the normal bosun's chair, like a kid's swing-seat, you sit about three feet below the hook or shackle on the line hauling you up. In Connemara the seat or the tiller is tied directly to the hook. You sit on that, and can reach three foot higher. We could now at least get to the work. It was still a fair old job, taking about an hour up there. I looked down at Sean helming before the sea to reduce the roll, but still the mast swung about. Every once in a while the wild swinging would slow down and for a moment I could get to work. The topping lift block had to be unshackled from the damaged metal band and attached to a rope strop made up to the mast-top. Easy to say, not so easy to do. When I was lowered to the deck I vomited everything I had eaten for two days over the side and continued to retch empty — but sufficient had been done. We were now in sailing shape again and the full mainsail was hoisted.

Some hours later an evening sunsight put us at 20° 50′ North, 18° West. We were far enough south to catch the trade wind. We altered course to the west and were now truly on our way.

Later that day we set to work on repairs. Colm, hanging over the stern his feet held, working on the damaged rudder. Johnny holds his harness line.

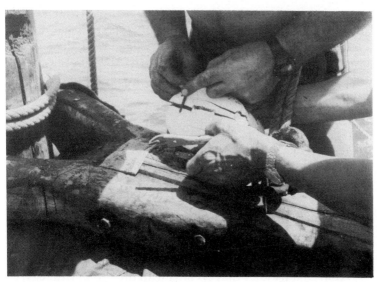

Rigging repairs: a damaged block

CHAPTER FIVE

Whales and Trades

ALL WINTER I had worked to get my Ham Radio Licence. I was now the holder of licence number EI 6GH, with the adjunct MM (maritime mobile) for the voyage's duration. It was 18.00 GMT on Wednesday, May 14. My hand lay poised over the morse key as the time came for our scheduled contact with EI 6BT, Jerry Cahill in Cork. I double-checked the set, frequency reading correct, SWR minimum, power output maximum and waited. The noise and interference was something terrible. There were about three other stations on the frequency, rattling out a staccato of morse. I sweated and stood by. 6BT was to call me. Suddenly a new sound joined the cacophony. I caught about half of it but knew we were on.

'Calling EI 6GH MM. This is EI 6BT. Please acknowledge'. 'EI 6BT. This is EI 6GH MM. Do you receive?' 'Roger, Roger', tapped out Jerry. We had contact but I felt way out of my depth. This was very different from the classes in Terenure College. Faintly from the radio set I heard a sweet Cork accent calling 'Echo India Six Gulf Hotel'. We were in business. I managed to get out our latitude and longitude, that we had got a pasting and were now OK. Then radio conditions closed in. However 6BT had acknowledged and we had set up our next schedule for Saturday next.

A radio contact later that evening with the UK Maritime Network was frustrating because of its excellence. Why could we not have had equally good contact earlier with Jerry? The network gave us some weather information they had and suggested we go a little further south. It was somewhat cloudy, but the wind was blowing for us so we continued as we were.

We had our first real meal that night, leaving us feeling content. Sean and Danny were on the ten to two a.m. watch and it being eleven I was for the sleeping bag.

The log reads as follows:

24.00 (Sean) distance 196 miles. Course 274 degrees Magnetic. Barometer 75.6. Cabin Temp. 22°C. Wind comes and goes. Overcast. Crescent moon. Balmy.

02.00 distance 205. Wind fresher. Bar./Temp. Steady.

05.35 (Kevin) 25 minutes to tot of whiskey . . .

10.00 (Paddy) 230 miles. 13 for watch. Wind from the east, a fitful force 2 to 4. Cloudy but warm. At eight Colm and myself put up the big jib and took the reefs out of the main. At nine the gaff jaws came away from the mast. With help from Danny and Sean, dropped main, refixed the gaff strap and raised sail again. Much usage of nails. Will the stock hold out?

18.00 274 miles (Johnny writes) at 15.30 I spotted what looked like a flock of translucent house sparrows, silvery and about forty in number. They were gliding about two feet over the water, with taut wings, in a north-easterly direction, into the wind. They splashed clumsily into the water about 40 yards abeam having crossed our bows. As they immediately disappeared I realised that they were flying fish. I later saw two more, much closer going in the same direction, ten or twelve inches long with outstretched fins along almost their entire length. Their backs seem to arch. While the wings don't appear to flap they can somehow steer to avoid wave tops.

Some cloud but mainly hot and sunny.

P.S. The flock of flying fish made a sound like the 'swish' of a bunch of cyclists at speed on a level road.

At ten o'clock on that Thursday night I wrote 'I have just finished a memorable watch, even if we did only ten miles. It

There was always an element of competition in doing a good watch run. The Walker distance log.

It wasn't all repairs, here Sean is cooking.

was very light to begin with. In fact Sean, after checking with me, went swimming. He dived in ahead from the bow to find the boat moving deceptively fast and had to swim hard to make the rubber tyre hanging over the side, at the stern'.

As darkness fell about 8.45 we could see a rain patch to the north of us and wished for the wind that must have been there. About nine a sudden wind shift and lift allowed us to gybe and reach away directly on our line to the west. We were on our course for the first time all day. Our evening sunsight gave us a day's run of 111 miles.

Danny has already finished reading his first book. He has the right idea — reading in his bunk. Reading on deck one gets through a page at most before blinking, nodding off or becoming otherwise distracted.

The moon is now in its third night and from its slender beginnings on Monday is now putting a fine shine on the water, when it gets through the clouds.

You would think that in fine weather you would have all the time in the world but it doesn't work out that way. After coming off watch this morning at ten I went to the bunk for a couple of hours, dozed, replaced a broken string on my guitar, got up and started playing. Inspired, or maybe the opposite, Colm took out his box. The box, accordion to you, had got a little damp and needed an outing. I had a bodhrán with me. Its skin, peculiarly, was very loose on its frame and needed a lot of rubbing to heat it to bring up the resonance. Johnny's set of Uilleann pipes seemed to have suffered nothing, but all of our fingers felt like sticks. Colm recorded some of our stuff for Radio na Gaeltachta, for whom he is doing a commentary. He is settling in very well, and getting the hang of steering *Saint Patrick*. He is tremendously enthusiastic.

Today I fitted a new electric light over the table. This transforms the reading and writing situation — and it has a switch that doesn't threaten to fall off every time you touch it. Batteries in one of our torches were replaced to-day. We also changed our first container of water. It had lasted three days. However, as for two of these we were being battered or were recovering from the effects and eating little or nothing, that water consumption would hardly be typical.

All bowels have now moved, I think. The calculation of toilet paper required was a new one — on which no guidance was available. 'What would we need for six weeks?' We allowed 1 metre of paper (over-generous I thought) per trip by 1 trip per day per man × 42 days × 6 men divided by 50 metres per roll. Multiply by a factor for losses due to a wetting by sea water and we took 12 rolls. And we have no newspaper delivery to make up any shortfall!

We have menus and cooking rotas worked out which have yet to be put into effect. The eating is still dictated by trying to use the fresh meat ahead of imminent decay. And meals are being prepared by individual initiative, mostly Sean's — and Danny's also, let it be said.

Keeping the cabin table clear of personal debris, sunglasses, lotions, books and all is gradually taking effect, with my threats to throw any offending items into the gash bucket — all taken in good part, I think.

Me to bunk now — 'oíche mhaith'. While I slept Danny wrote 'an oíche is aoibhne fós, roinnt réaltóga — loinnir na gealaí lag sóilsiu ar thosadh an bháid. Ó mhéanoíche amach an spéir clúdaithe le scamaill agus an ghaoith ag neartú'.

I had hoped to improve on my speaking of Irish. This should have been easy, what with Colm and Danny being native speakers. Early on I could see that it wouldn't work out. Danny as a youngster in Ballyferriter had had a surfeit of earnest learners staying in his family house and ever since has an aversion to the language learning — not to the language or the use of it, far from it. He would have helped me but in our cramped world I felt that nothing non-essential should be asked of anyone. Colm, my watch-mate, would have happily spoken and taught Irish to me. But again as a pair we were more at home in English. The crack, and the conversation, the phrase and the nod were the cornerstone of our social community. Whatever was best for this was best for the voyage. By and large I let my ambition for Irish to one side. Colm and Danny used it

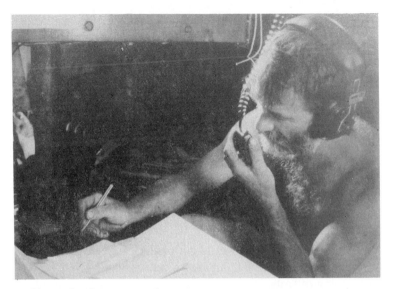

Paddy on the short-wave radio

Overhauling our hand pumps. Colm's preventative maintenance kept our machinery in good order.

all the time, at the speed of light it seemed. Colm, who had spent years in England, reckoned that Danny spoke beautiful Irish like poetry.

4 a.m. Friday May 16th. Stars gone, overcast, warm, dark, wind not constant and hard to keep to course. Very gentle swell.

At six a.m., the end of their watch, Johnny wrote:

For exceptional devotion to duty we award ourselves the 'Jameson Memorial Prize'. As Colm is actually asleep it seems a shame to wake him for his watch. At about 5.15 a plane went over, not very high and not a jet. Possibly a military transport to Ascension Island.

It was 6.30 before Colm and I got on deck. There wasn't a lot going on. A fickle breeze from astern caused an alternate filling and flapping of sails. We would make better speed if we were to take the breeze on our beam and steer to the north west but we had better stay to the south. I would try on the radio to-day to find out if the trade winds were blowing at lower latitudes. There was a sailing boat with radio a few days ago, two hundred miles to the south of us. We would try to contact her to see what wind she is getting.

The sun rose in style at 7.30 but it was hard to enjoy it. Oh for a wind, or even a breeze! Eventually I could stand it no more, started our engine and steered to the south-west where hopefully we would find wind.

For a few hours we motored at low throttle in a broad and flat Atlantic. The cabin temperature was 25 degrees and outside it was hot. In the early afternoon a light north-easter ruffled the surface. The engine went off and the sails went up. Unfortunately in raising the big calico jib it caught in the anchor winch, putting a six-foot tear in it. After a brief lesson in the herringbone stitch Colm worked his way along it. Kevin had a sextant lesson on noon sights. We unlashed the anchor from the deck and stowed it below and the afternoon went drifting by.

Seventy yards off a pair of huge fish came up, nearly out of

72

the water. 'Lads, lads, there are whales!' They were about thirty feet long, moving slowly in the opposite direction to us, raising about half of their bodies out of the water, as they lifted up and down. On each upper side was a large swept-back curved fin. Underneath they were white. Killer whales — they were gone before we had time to be worried.

22.00 A wind came up from the north-west direction a couple of hours ago and gave us pleasant close-hauled sailing in a flat sea. Then the light over the compass packed up. Colm put in a replacement bulb which worked. Now it has gone again and so have our port and starboard navigation lights.

It didn't greatly matter that our green and red sidelights weren't working. After all the shipping traffic wasn't exactly nose to tail and the whales, if there were any about, would hardly be intimidated by our navigational right of way. But the absence of the compass light was a nuisance. It meant that the man on the helm operated with a flashlamp to see the compass. The sky was largely clear but what cloud there was seemed to be blotting out any stars which might be useful to steer by. John Masefield, you were quite right:

> All I want is a tall ship
> And a star to steer her by.

Colm later got all the lights working again — by which time the cloud had cleared from the horizon ahead and you could again steer by a star.

We never bothered with star sights, mostly because they require more knowledge than I have and also because you need continual practice. The sights have to be taken within a short duration at twilight when the stars are up but the horizon is still visible. In any event in the part of the world we were sailing we would be unlucky not to get sunsights.

This was Friday night. Our distance logged at midnight was 369 miles, not great after over four days out. But then, what harm. All sails were drawing lightly and we were getting 14 to 15 miles a watch. At six a.m. Johnny wrote, 'This is great

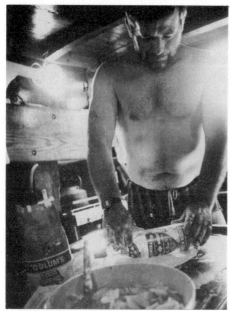

Domesticity itself,
Colm baking.

Johnny at the cabin table

shooting star territory — they seem more frequent and also to last longer before burning up'.

On Saturday morning a breeze came up from the north-west. We tried sailing, the wind was west by north-west actually, about force 3. Yes we could close reach at a reasonable rate towards the south-west.

In selecting material for our breakfast, fried egg sandwiches and tomatoes, it came to light that our greens, the bananas and tomatoes, were ripening far too quickly. We already had the odd discard — although Sean would usually be standing by to salvage any possible edible portion for later use.

Two p.m. brought us a $20\frac{1}{4}$ mile watch — our first 20-miler. We reduced the big jib to the working jib and reefed the main. This left us a little undercanvassed but the practice was useful to knock a few of the wrinkles out of our sail changing drill. More pumping was needed now as we were driving harder.

Sean made a log entry about a flying fish thirteen inches long he had seen. There was some lively debate about the validity of making a log entry of this nature without supporting corroboration!

For days we had seen occasional floating balloon-like objects on the sea surface, about six inches diameter, translucent and with streamers below. Johnny had no trouble in identifying them as the caul in which sharks are born, Maiden's Purses. He even had the name they went by. Nothing would do him but to try and bring one aboard. No one else was that keen, not knowing how the Daddy sharks might respond to this. In any event Colm made a net with which Johnny tried his hand, to no avail.

That Saturday night we had a radio schedule and I prepared the essentials of our news.

'QTH (location) at GMT 17.00 24° 27' North. 21° 30' West.
Days' runs last three days   Thursday 111 miles
                                     Friday 86 miles
                                     Saturday 94 miles
All well and going well'.

Radio conditions were excellent and we had a great chat with Jerry 6BT and a pal of his, Tony 2CV. Tony works with the *Cork Examiner* and was fascinated with our story. Following this radio link, they did a piece on us. We gave them the up-to-date story down to what we were about to have for the dinner — omitting that there was a bottle of best Canary Island White being landed on the table. That might have sounded too soft altogether!

With the warm conditions now, it was no trouble to do a couple of hours at a time on the tiller. Colm took it from six to eight, while I took a sunsight and plotted it and then spent over an hour on the radio. Our mileage on the Walker log gave us a day's run of 94 miles, but our sunsight fix gave us only 76 on the chart — something of a let-down. However if the present sailing conditions kept up that would be, as Danny might say, 'a matter of nothing'.

In fact on the last watch with the wind veered round to north-east and more on our quarter we did 19¾ miles without effort, even though the wind would regularly fall light for five or ten minutes at a time before coming up again.

This was an entirely different evening from any before. Up to now, the clouds on the horizon at sunset would tend to be spread and cloud over the sky for a while after dark. This evening the sun set in a golden circle with a half-moon directly overhead. Long after Venus shone bright in the western sky a red glow reflected off small scattered clouds hanging stationary in the sky — almost ethereal in its beauty.

I had all this beauty to myself because my philistinic mates were engrossed below, playing cards. In anticipation of our eventual landfall the stakes were in US dollars. Johnny was $2 up, with Danny also featuring on the credit side.

I had started reading a John B. Keane book (not on watch of course!) about a north Kerry matchmaker — I would say a cross between John B. himself and our own Danny. I worked in Kerry myself as a young civil engineer and remember some gems from that county. I had bought a bed in Listowel, an expensive one I thought. 'Does it have any sort of guarantee?' I innocently enquired. The man from McKenna's looked at me, sort of quiz-zically, and said, 'You must be expecting a lot of traffic over it, boy?'

Somewhere in our preparatory reading there was a piece about sunburn, recommending the wearing of pyjamas as a preventative. The result of that is that both Kevin and Sean had this pyjama-clad Viet Cong look. Colm and Kevin, the only non-bearded faces to start with, were now at the itchy stage.

I was in the cabin after my last night watch and was pouring a tot of whiskey into my glass. We had brought only a couple of bottles of whiskey but had eight bottles of poteen, five of which Colm described as 'speisialta', being almost a year old. The others were good but had an age measured in weeks.

We had no live music to-day but did hear from 'Cork' radio that Communions were on there and that 'Self-Aid' was going on all day on TV.

Sunday for me was wash day. It should also of course have been prayer-day but I'm sorry to say that I saw no evidence of any special observance. Where was the piety so much in evidence the previous Sunday as we bent the knee in the church at Los Cristianos? We had plenty to be thankful for, having come so handily through the weather we'd had. Like many we pray only to ask, rarely to thank.

The pep talk before the off had included a few comments on personal cleanliness. I wasn't the one to preach. However the possibility of spread of infection, not to speak of distasteful body odours in confined quarters, was mentioned. Personal hygiene was praised as a *very good thing*. Colm had taken this to heart, and was to be seen on the foredeck most mornings giving himself a thorough salt-water going over, head to toe — commendable indeed, far beyond the call of duty. A good friend and dentist, Dermot Sullivan, had spoken to me on toothcare — not just for the voyage, but for 'the voyage of life' as he put it. I had accordingly equipped myself with dental floss for the between-teeth cleanout. Johnny had borrowed twelve inches of this, and knotted the ends together to make an endless circle. I have to say that such frugality is to be admired and encouraged.

77

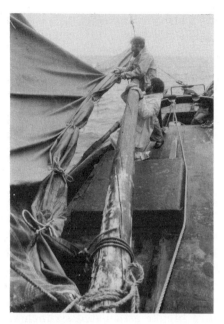

Reefing could be hard work

On this Sunday morning I proceeded to give myself an on-deck wash using a bar of salt-water soap. I had been given this years ago, by my mother-in-law Kathleen, God bless her, looking after her sailor son-in-law.

Now fresh water for washing is not on, or at most is limited to a cup or so. And here was I on deck, covered with lather, at least a gallon of hot water in the bucket, liberally splashing it all over myself, the deck and all. Dark murmurings from the lads. 'I didn't know we could break out the fresh water', said Kevin. Sean, who had been carefully quartermastering and stock-taking the water, spoke out: 'I wasn't consulted about this'. I had soap in my hair and eyes and didn't know what they were on about. Only when I had rinsed off with a bucket of water from over the side and could see again did the penny drop.

Not a fish had yet succumbed to the tempting bait offered by Kevin on the fishing line. During the morning the swivel was found to be jammed. This may or may not have made the lure less life-like. The swivel was fixed and a new bait put on, the 'wobbler', as we called it, a lifelike articulated six-inch fish (plastic, of course) with hooks attached.

Our masthead Irish Cruising Club burgee had somehow survived the knock-down when other masthead 'paraphernalia' had succumbed. Like the Fastnet Light, which features on it, it had withstood the storm but was now beginning to wear thin. We took it down to give it a rest and put up an ordinary flag instead to show the wind direction.

During the day the sailing was making about 17 miles to the watch. Johnny produced from the depths of his luggage a rich and moist fruit cake baked by Nuala Walsh, who, having married into a family of voracious eaters, matched quality with quantity. Even with the slices cut to doorstep dimensions we got several days out of that cake.

Later Colm put a message, worded in Irish and English, in a bottle and despatched it over the side. It reminded me of a Glencullen stonemason I knew who did restoration work on a number of old ruined churches around south County Dublin. He always built into a wall of each church a bottle with the

Sun sights were taken twice daily.

names of the men doing the restoration and the date.

The calculations that evening showed a discrepancy of 30 miles as between our Walker-logged distance and our charted distance by sunsights. As it was in our favour I wasn't unduly worried. But the day before there had been an 18 mile difference in the other direction. As there was still 2,300 miles to Bermuda there was plenty of time to sharpen the navigator's pencil.

––––––––––

'Quick, quick, there's a fish on the line'.

Well, you'd think we had never seen a fish before in our lives there was such excitement. It was a 'biggie' to judge by the action on the line. Everyone crowded the stern armed with gaffs, Colm's net and curiosity as the unfortunate fish was hauled in and despatched to its heaven. A dolphin fish we thought it was, about 7 pounds, and just the job for the lunch tomorrow.

The day ended well. Not only had we caught a fish, had some cake, fixed the fuse to the VHF and launched a bottle but the last watch was $21\frac{3}{4}$ miles. The moon rose lighting up sea and sails. There was a feeling of old times to be knocking off 20-mile-plus watches again after those slow 12 to 15ers.

The distance to go is now 900 miles to Mid-Atlantic, neatly identified by a fold in the chart, then 930 miles to 60°W 25°N and then 500 miles North-west to Bermuda. It's much too early to be looking so far ahead but mid-Atlantic by this day week certainly looks on to-night as we are powering along.

At that stage we had run 574 miles on the Walker log so it certainly was too soon to speculate. The log line had been damaged and shortened in the tangle after the knock down, so its accuracy was suspect anyway. We took down the foresail. It was doing nothing blanketed behind the mainsail, as we were more or less directly downwind.

Pumping was featuring again, unfortunately, in our activity.

We were having to pump between 100 and 200 strokes each hour. That in itself was no particular problem. With our Whale 25 handpump it was probably about 50 gallons an hour, taking less than five minutes to get rid of it. But there was the danger that it might get worse. There were two planks on the waterline, port side, that had shown signs of springing when we were doing repairs in Tenerife. Each plank was showing an edge about $\frac{1}{4}$-inch proud of its adjacent plank. There wasn't much that could be done about it except to drive in some additional spikes to hold the planks in place and then caulk away. As we were on the starboard tack these planks were now about a foot underwater. At least I knew where to look first if the water intake got out of hand.

To-day was the last day of our week. This was very significant. We can now renew from 'central stores', the contents of our snack drawer, containing Mars bars and raisins. Last week's Mars are long gone, although the raisins are still to the good. Our large sacks of carrots and onions appear undiminished in size. We will have to invent ways to resolve this. If freshwater supplies look good a light freshwater clothes wash may be on the cards shortly — underpants last.

We will be changing watch to-night and one of these days we will have to move the time on the cabin clock as we make to the west. It's now getting bright at eight in the morning and dark about ten. Maybe to-night we'll change to give daylight 7 a.m. to 9 p.m. The separate quartz navigation clock, set to Greenwich Mean Time, will of course stay put.

The cooking rota was now in effect. The dreaded day had come when myself and Colm were on. Colm had no cooking experience, he said, and my talent in this area was not highly regarded. I was determined to upgrade my reputation. Our cookery book suggested just the opportunity — baked stuffed tomatoes with spiced tuna. We had plenty of big tomatoes, we had tins of tuna, and an oven to cook it all. That's what we did and from Sean came the ultimate accolade. He had no need to rinse his plate, and he initiated a discussion on which spices we had used.

83

This one was, we
think, a
Barracuda.

A dolphin fish.
These are very
lively on the line,
but their size
when we did land
one was often
somewhat
disappointing.

We pumped 205 strokes, 230 strokes and then 150 strokes in the next three hours. Our charted day's run was plotted at 134 miles. Fantastic. The pilot chart shows a westerly current of 0.4 knots in this area which would have contributed about eight of those miles. We had a sense of elation at our second day's excellent run. This was the wind and current we had come for.

In the evening we went to cook our fine fish, only to discover that it already had maggots. The next one we catch will go straight into the pan. Danny dumped the fish, only to be reprimanded by Sean. 'You could have cooked that. A few maggots would be no harm.'

During the preparation of the (alternative) evening meal Sean noticed that the stitching of the mainsail at the lower end by the shrouds was gone, and a split about a foot long was opening up. Quick as we could, we reefed, to take the torn seam out of the line of fire, and then the cooking resumed.

The Erin goulash dinner turned out very, very salty. I had made it on sea-water, but unfortunately the makers had already included all the salt necessary. My earlier fine culinary efforts were quickly forgotten and my former reputation was restored.

9 p.m. Kevin pumped 364 strokes.

'What? Are you sure?' 'Did you count each half stroke as one?' Kevin was in no doubt. '364 full strokes', he said.

We could have a problem on our hands but an hour later the pumping was down to a 150 level so we relaxed again.

Looking at the log I saw that Colm had, a little before midnight written in: 'An bhfuil an bád sí ag seóladh linn?' (Is the ghost boat sailing with us?) That sounded a little creepy. Colm told me the story.

'In Connemara, when *Saint Patrick*, or *Bád Chonroí* as she was also called, was working, she was always regarded as not only a very good boat but also as a lucky boat. One of the stories was that she had a ghost ship which sailed in company with her. In times of trouble this ghost ship would sometimes be seen. It was always regarded as a good sign. It meant that you were being looked after'.

Colm had got this story from his father. They came from Camus, on the innermost end of Rosmuc Bay. *Saint Patrick* spent most of her working life based in Garrivan, Rosmuc, and the watch passed easily as we chatted about the Hookers, the *bádóirí* (boatmen) and the work they did. Colm's family moved to Rathcairn, Co. Meath when he was fourteen, along with twenty-four other Irish speaking Connemara families. Thirty years on, Rathcairn is as lively, as Irish speaking and as prosperous as anywhere in Ireland, but Colm misses living by the sea. However he was getting enough of it now to do him a while.

On Tuesday I looked around our food stocks. It seemed as if there were many items likely to be untouched. I gazed at a couple of catering-size jars of Heinz ploughman's pickle. It would take a lot of curry to make an impression on that. The 'long-life' milk was a treat: we had brought 2 dozen litres and they were going at about one a day. I saw macaroni 'to beat the band' — as yet untouched. We were still working on some German-type brown bread that Sean had unearthed in Los Cristianos, which could, at best, be described as 'serviceable'.

At 1 p.m. the wind was logged at force 6. For curiosity I looked up the description in the Almanac of force 6. 'Large waves begin to form. The white foam crests are more extensive everywhere. Probably some spray.' Yes, this was about force six all right. But it makes all the difference if you are going with it or against.

As the seas built up we couldn't steer directly downwind for fear of gybing, especially as it grew dark. We went 15 or 20 degrees to the south of our course. The bait on the line was changed after the fishing line tangled with the log line, and they wrapped about a hundred and one times around each other. Below, the evening was undramatic. There was reading, quiet chat, repeating of yesterday's jokes and not a lot of fresh wit. From above I heard that the compass light had packed up, again, and this after its fine fix-up job to-day, even packing and sealing it with silicone-grease. Luckily we have plenty of batteries for the flashlamp.

Stop rocking the boat! Johnny up the mast with Sean, Colm and Danny below.

At 10 p.m. Johnny and Kevin noted, 'took last tot of whiskey — on to the real stuff now, the poitín'.

With over eight hundred miles gone a routine has set in. We were to have rotated bunks yesterday but all, even Kevin with his home on the wine cellar and Danny in the hatch bunk, expressed a preference to stay put. As I write Danny has just transferred, for this watch, to my bunk. Even for a stoic such as himself getting a third bucketful of water on to his face as he lay in his bunk was not conducive to a restful sleep.

Not a harsh or an angry word has been spoken. A very easy atmosphere prevails and looks like continuing. The closest thing to discord is in relation to Sean's very careful approach to disposal of waste and left-over food. Danny says he is even afraid to throw out the contents of the gash bucket now, after the looks from Sean over dumping the fish full of maggots.

Wednesday brought continued pumping, now averaging over 200 strokes an hour. The work in pumping was no hardship but the rate of intake was something we should be doing something about. We had looked at the inside planking where it was easily visible, including the area of the two suspect planks. However all of this was only about half of the total. Between ballast, fixtures, bunks and heavy stowed gear a lot of the planking was only accessible from inside with major efforts. For the present it was far easier to keep pumping.

Shortly after nine in the morning it began to actually *rain*. This brought a full complement on deck, and I think I detected a little nostalgia for our Irish weather. It was over before we had a chance to let it wash us down. The morning stayed cloudy with the wind and seas gone down. The day before it had got up to force seven or so and was a little on the wild side for comfort, even going downwind. Danny transferred to my bunk again. Colm's quarters on the other hand are like home from home. He put up some polythene to deflect the drips and fixed a canvas curtain to keep out the hatch-originating water.

I gave myself a good freshwater wash using a cup of water

and feel the better for it. It's amazing how far a cup can go, if judiciously used. First I rinsed my contact lenses and put them on, the better to see. Then I flossed my teeth, washed them and rinsed out being careful not to wash the tooth-brush in the mug. Did you know that right handed people have better teeth in the left hand side of the mouth because of the way they wash them? With soap and scrubber do the face and neck, under the arms — very important, and lastly the crotch which tends to get very sweaty in the heat. Towel off, comb hair, underpants and shorts on again and the day is at your command.

As the morning passed the cloud began to clear. I had been concerned that we might not be able to get a sunsight. I had taken none the day before.

We changed up to the big jib and I missed the noon sight by an hour. I had forgotten to make an allowance for the hour we had moved the cabin clock. The sight I took an hour after local noon showed that the sun was still almost directly overhead but already bearing 258 degrees.

Still we pumped and sailed. Colm got the compass light going, finding nothing obviously wrong. At 18.00 hrs. GMT we made radio schedule with Jerry, and gave him our estimated position. He would later be in contact with Mary Barry. He told us that news was just in that a sailing ship, *The Pride of Baltimore*, had gone down during a storm in the west Atlantic, with four men lost and ten saved.

This sent a chill through us. This ship was, like ourselves, bound for Opsail in New York. But she was a big capable vessel, over a hundred and thirty feet long. Her master, Armin Etsaesser, had shown me round her last year, when she had visited Cork. She was only nine years old and in the best of condition. What had happened?

'Did it go on reefs or rocks?' we asked on the radio. 'Did they have any names of those lost or saved?'

The information was sparse. As far as was known they were well out to sea, somewhere off to the south-west of Bermuda. This made it worse. It was not far from the area we were making for.

Fine weather activity: Colm giving himself a shower; Kevin washing clothes.

CHAPTER SIX

A Mid-Atlantic Party

WE MADE few direct remarks about the *Pride of Baltimore*. However, the effect of the news was noticeable in many small ways. The boat was pumped more often, and more thoroughly. Even though it was late evening I set to stitching the seam of the mainsail. Any dark clouds were scrutinised that little more thoroughly for squalls to come. Later that night, possibly forcing ourselves, we had music in the cabin. Box, whistle and guitar and Kevin playing bodhrán because Danny begged out saying 'he had hurt his wrist'.

At six in the morning Danny wrote: 'Tá an caravan ciúin' (All quiet in the caravan). This used to annoy Colm, Danny calling the 'bád mór' a 'caravan'.

On Thursday morning we passed the 1,000 mile mark without much comment. Colm was busy most of the day over-hauling the hand pumps. We had one always set up for use, and two spares. I took a morning sight, plotted it and set the alarm clock to ring in time for the noon sight. The morning longitude seemed too good to be true so I held fire on announcing the result until I would get confirmation of our westing from an evening sight. As I waited for local noon I gazed over the side wondering where was all the water getting into the boat? And how were our sunsights giving consistently greater distances than the trailing log? Was it ocean current? We should be getting about ten or twelve miles a day from that. Maybe the log is under-reading. We have another trailing log. We must do a check with that. Anyway, what matters is our charted position from sunsights. The sun does not lie!

The sorting and disposal of bad fruit continues. It is disappointing how much has to be dumped. In Tenerife we should have tried to buy the stuff greener. Johnny finds the drinking water unpalatable and talks about boiling it for twenty minutes but to tell the truth, I see no problem. We have purifying tablets but I see no need to use them. As I said before there is a slight taste, but you'd get used to that.

The VHF antenna, damaged in the knockdown, now went altogether and that hurts because, as far as I know, it is one thing we cannot fix ourselves. However I'll ask the lads in Cork about it next Saturday.

Insurrection nearly broke out around four over the lunch, or rather, the lack of it. Colm and myself were on cooking rota, and we had had a big breakfast just before one. I had asked around about forgoing lunch but apparently my sample enquiry had been unrepresentative. A quick dive for three tins of potato salad, some tinned tuna and peas, with Rioja Rosé, saved the day. Later I threw out the sack of carrots as they were rotten. The bloody things must have been a month old when we bought them.

'Is a "pionntadóir" a pint drinker?' asked Johnny over the dinner that night. We had covered 113 miles for the day and we were all in fine fettle as the miles rolled on over a flat sea. Danny was describing a man in Clare who was brought up to court for taking women in a van round to bachelor farmers. 'I think I hear a van pulling up outside' said Kevin, keeping a straight face, as we rolled round the table in hysterics.

Sean was trying to read Hans Küng through all of this.

After midnight I made contact with the U.S. Maritime Network on 14,313 mHz. They were all over the place. Central America, Santiago, Chile and into the Pacific, taking calls and passing on messages for 'Maritime Mobile and Deployed

We came upon a floating radio beacon. A frenzy of 'stripomania' ensued. Its batteries were long since flat.

Swimming in water 3 miles deep. Sometimes the trade winds would fall flat and that would be swimming time. We saw no sharks.

Military'. They didn't seem at all surprised or impressed at hearing from us.

At four Danny noted, 'Johnny éirithe don céad uair roimhis Kevin' — another first. Not that I should throw stones; Colm was always on deck before me. I would always have to check the log, the bilge water, the kettle or anything.

'Paddy, there's something up ahead', Kevin said to me, as I dozed the last hour of my off-watch in the bunk on Friday. It was 9.30 on the cabin clock as I went for the open hatch, grabbing the binoculars from their shelf as I went.

'You won't need those', said Johnny. 'It's just up ahead'. There, fifty metres on our bow, was a floating buoy of some sort with a mast about twelve feet out of the water.

The day was well warmed up although Kevin and Johnny still wore oilskins from their 6 a.m. start. The wind was a light force 3 from astern and the sea was quiet. As we rounded up, the lads peeling off their oilies, dammit didn't we miss it as it slid by, out of reach of the boathook. Round we went again, paying out the mainsheet, gybing and then heading up to it, more accurately this time. A grab with the boat-hook brought it alongside. There was nothing obviously radioactive or explosive about it. The stick appeared to be like a radio aerial. Up she was lifted, little crabs crawling all over it, and we laid it on deck. As Kevin described the scene — 'in five minutes, in a frenzy of "stripo-mania" we had it all apart and, like a Christmas toy, now didn't know what to do with it'. It turned out to be a radio buoy with a transmitter run off a small battery, long dead. It was dated 1981. With wind and current it could only have come from the east.

Johnny proceeded to salvage an impressive array of bits and pieces, stainless steel nuts and bolts, pieces of rope and a 12-volt, 350 milliamp bulb. This bulb actually worked when we tested it. A treasure trove of useless junk, except for the rope from which Johnny later made a dozen five-foot lashings. And we had great fun keeping the crabs from crawling into the bilges. A crab farm in the bilges we did not need.

In manoeuvring for the buoy we had started the engine but

couldn't get forward gear. Colm later spent the most of three hours doing a repair job on the gear cable and, fair play to him, got it working again. Kevin spotted under the boat a couple of dozen striped fish which we decided were 'pilot' fish. They didn't respond in a positive way to the 'feathers' with which Kevin immediately tried to tempt them — no result.

For some days Johnny had been vainly attempting to net what he called Mermaid's Purses, or was it Maiden's Purses? Later this day he caught one. It looked something like a jelly-fish, with tentacles of brilliant colour varying from white through to deep blue. Johnny put it in a plastic container, along with some crabs, which he now referred to as his aquarium.

The day was hot, the hottest yet. We put a bucket of water by the hatch so you could cool your feet in it as you passed.

And then there was the fish — a possible 'barracuda' or maybe a 'yahoo'. It certainly had a mouthful of vicious-looking teeth. It had been on the line for hours, by the stretched look of him when we brought him in. Kevin cut it into fillets and contributed him to the lunch. But we really needed something bigger on the line.

With all the goings-on I missed the noon sight (again) to-day. With the sun almost overhead a sight at actual local noon is the only one of any use for getting an accurate latitude. We have been creeping a little to the north, sixty miles in three days, and we don't want to find ourselves out of the trade wind area. Our position this evening was put at 36° 25' west, 25° 12' north. We have 1,113 miles showing on the log.

All in all a very good day, buoyant spirits, no wine with lunch but two bottles later, and we started baking our own bread — a great improvement.

The wind on Saturday ranged from light to none at all. We used the engine now and again to keep moving. Johnny, Sean and myself had a swim. The pumping must have been badly neglected at one stage as it needed 850 strokes to clear the bilge. That was about one ton of water on the loose.

It now appears that on Monday evening we will celebrate our arrival at Mid-Atlantic. Sean will cook and all must perform a turn — to a very exclusive audience.

That Saturday evening the lads in Cork told us how we could improvise an aerial for the VHF from a length of wire. We had music on deck and set-dancing lessons from Colm. The moon rose on our stern in a golden ball, lighting the edges of the clouds with a silver trimming.

Sunday began with a fickle breeze from the east, rising occasionally to all of a force 3. The boat would then heel and start a bow wave, only to slow to almost nothing, it seemed, as the bow wave died, but ripples from the stern continued. This, in daylight, might be called a swimming wind, where you dive in ahead off the bow, swim like blazes for ten or twelve strokes and find that the stern is already abeam. Then make a grab at the tyre we hang out when swimming, and you realize that even going slowly there is forward movement in it. It is a matter of the height from which the sea is viewed.

'Cigar agus Poitin', to finish my watch. A comparison later between the Walker logs showed that the one we had been using was under-reading by six miles in a hundred. That explained a lot of the navigational discrepancies.

During the morning Johnny's trousers went overboard while he was washing them. Quickly we gybed round into the wind and effected a gallant rescue of the britches, just as they were about to sink. The wind, which felt inconsequential going before it, was fresh enough when we rounded into it.

A ship passed five miles away to our south. We hastily made up a VHF aerial of sorts with a piece of clothes-hanger and managed to make contact. She was *Santa Rosa* and she gave us her position. Our longitude was spot on but our latitude was way out, about thirty miles — not good. At least we have our VHF in working order again.

Oh Lord, who otherwise are so kind to us, would you please raise the wind speed 5 knots and while you are at it bring it round to the north-east where it is supposed to be?

We had a setback to our stock of poitín tonight when one

bottle was found to have leaked empty. A pity about that, but we are not short. It's great to have something to look forward to on the long night watch. We don't bother with oilskins at all now and even at night the deck is warm on the bare feet.

On Monday morning it was found that the fishing line had an octopus tentacle impaled on it. Kevin got a sting from a sucker while he was removing it. We wondered if we had had a full octopus on the line — we must have had. To judge by the size of the tentacle, it must have been a fair old specimen.

During the day we indulged in a little scientific activity to determine the gain or loss in sailing off-course but faster. Our conclusion was that it was worth while sailing up to 20 degrees off to keep the headsails full.

That afternoon the port lower shroud parted where it was swaged into an eye round the mast. Johnny went up with a jury shroud of 2¼″ Courlene which when set up looked good. After all for years *Saint Patrick*, like all the Hookers, had rope shrouds.

The log was somewhat bare of comment for a while thereafter. We were at 42 degrees west and it was party time — for five out of six of us at any rate.

At eleven o'clock Kevin wrote:

This is going to be a long watch. The half-way party was great crack but it is not so easy to follow it with a four-hour stint. The highlight was some superb cuisine from Sean, well complemented by generous measures of the good wine. This mellowed the company considerably. The best party piece was undoubtedly Johnny's take-off of our radio contacts with the lads in Cork - better than the real thing...No hats or streamers but what a night. The Rathcairn dried mackerel is certainly an acquired taste - but well done, Sean. Your snores now cannot but be deleterious to the fabric of the boat.

At 2 a.m. Kevin and Johnny gratefully hit the bunk as Colm and I took over. For the first time in many weeks I had a reminder of what a hangover felt like.

97

Looking aft towards the hatch.

Happy times. This was the night of Colm's birthday. Here he cuts the cake — one candle only.

The classic sailing ship route westward from Europe to the eastern United States is given succinctly in *Ocean Passages for the World*. This volume is based on centuries of experience, thousands of years in the case of the Arab world. Its advice should be disregarded at peril.

'Proceed at latitude 25 North and do not turn to the northward until a longitude of 60 West be attained', it says. Adhering to this would add several hundred miles to the straight-line distance. The recommended route would take us virtually around two sides of a triangle, but presumably the sailing winds would be better. We would take this course but might short-cut it somewhat. We had an engine, which could push us through the calms, but our diesel supply was limited. We would have to use it sparingly and judiciously.

Maybe we should have had our party earlier because with it came better winds. Thank you, Lord, for answering our prayer.

Our position now on the chart of the Atlantic Ocean was closer to Venezuela than to the United States. In fact if we were to ease our sheets only a little and steer off to the south-west we could be in Trinidad or Tobago in ten or twelve days. The islands of the West Indies were even closer. We sailed through the night, in silence mostly, making good time. The rate of pumping, it seemed, rose with the wind, although no one logged their count of strokes. Later the wind lightened and we steered a little north to maintain speed.

In the morning Sean had just gone up on the helm when Danny in the cabin said quietly:

'Wait and see what he wants this time'. A few minutes passed.

'Danny, could you get me up my sunglasses?'

We hadn't noticed that Sean, when he went to the helm, had always forgotten something. Danny, his watchmate, regarded it as a joke, but one that was now wearing somewhat thin.

As the day passed the wind improved again and so did our spirits. We composed fictitious telegrams:

'*Saint Patrick* arrived Venezuela stop Details earliest stop'.

However, all this pumping was no joke. As soon as conditions allowed we would see what could be done.

That evening and all through the night clouds hid the sky, with particularly dark ones here and there. The ship was pulling well, over twenty miles to each watch. The seas were moderate. Occasionally we would catch the top of a bigger sea and surf for a few seconds before resuming at normal speed. When the jib would flap, a shudder would run from the bowsprit through the hull, but though we were used to that by now, we still didn't like it.

Mid-morning, Wednesday 28 May saw us hauling in the fishing line to bring a fine dolphinfish aboard. The outlook for the day's diet had taken a distinct turn for the better. Colm baked two apple pies with professional aplomb. He insisted that this was his first effort at baking. The results belied it.

With eleven hundred miles to go to Bermuda we did some calculations on our diesel stock and how much motoring we could afford to do. We had ten five-gallon containers of diesel left, each one being good for thirty-three miles on the Walker Log. That had to be all right unless we were very unlucky indeed with the wind. However we would shortly be going through the Horse Latitudes. This was an area north of the trade wind zone, subject to long calms. Here the old sailing ships were often forced to drive their horses overboard to lighten ship in order to keep moving: better to lose the horses than that all should starve. Dawn on Thursday brought a slight ripple on the sea but the occasional breeze was nothing that we could use to sail effectively. While the engine was running we used the big belt-driven pump to clear the bilge.

Apart from having to keep diesel for an emergency, like 'man-overboard' or being caught in a gale off a lee-shore, we also had to save some to be able to run the big pump were we to spring a plank or take heavy water aboard. Idly I doodled various sums relating to diesel usage, put them away and went up to the foredeck, clipped on my harness and fell asleep wrapped in the calico jib.

Later in the morning we had a general work session during which we actually did some preventative maintenance. Danny and myself did a job on the transom where the tiller was rubbing, Sean and Johnny fixed the topping lift at the mast-head, Colm and Kevin overhauled the anchor winch. Then on the impulse I thought that we had better stop beating around the bush and do something about our major potential problem. After all, we were over a thousand miles from land and our boat had a leak. I got out face-mask, flippers and snorkel. We stopped the engine, looked around for signs of sharks and over the side I went. Colm, a trained diver, which I am not, went in the water too to keep watch for sharks. Up and down the length of the hull I swam prodding the seams with a screwdriver. On each dive I could go about half the length of the boat, examining one seam, provided I didn't delay in my prodding. After about half an hour of this I could find nothing wrong. All the seams appeared tight. Mind you, the putty had been washed out of many of the underwater seams and the Tenerife caulking cotton was showing white, but that wouldn't have been a cause of leaking.

'Maybe the offending seam only opens up under stress of sailing?' Maybe, but there was no way anyone could be diving under the hull while we were moving. The sterntube had been checked and tightened on the inside. The engine cooling water intake had been examined. There seemed nowhere else to look when, on an afterthought, I swam round to the transom. There was our problem, obvious as you like. Where the joint between the rudder post and the transom had been caulked, about twelve inches of caulking cotton was hanging loose. The loosening of the rudder in the knockdown had shaken up the caulking. With lump hammer and caulking iron it took only a couple of dives by Colm and myself to hammer it into place again. We didn't do the full length, both sides, but we now knew where to tackle the problem again if we had to.

During all this the breeze filled in, so when all were aboard again we got up sail and by steering north-west to bring the wind on our quarter were able to make moderate speed. At 4 p.m. the temperature was 33 degrees in the cabin, 31 degrees on deck in the shade and the sea 25 degrees.

About this time we first began to notice the seaweed, Sargasso weed. About every 100 yards or so we would pass a ball of this, about one foot in diameter. We were entering the edge of the Sargasso Sea.

At 9 p.m. that evening a ship bound from Venezuela to Liverpool wished us 'very well trip' and told us that there would be more wind to-morrow. Good. The position she gave confirmed that we were still slipping slightly to the north, 47° 27' West, 25° 33' North.

The next day did bring better winds, southerly force 3 and 4, for us. But the bad news was that we found our remaining eggs to have gone to the bad. There were only a couple of dozen left, and they were quietly disposed of. In the following days the wind came and went. On average it was all right as we always topped a hundred a day but going back over our log for this period it shows an amalgam of course changes, sail changes, optimism and pessimism as the wind toyed with us.

The Sargasso weed became denser. It was now all about, spaced about five yards in each direction. You could see it for a depth of at least ten feet. Kevin had had to give up the fishing. Every few hours the Walker log would get fouled in weed and have to be taken in and freed.

The pumping required had reduced by about half and I was sure that a more thorough job wearing air bottles would reduce it by half again. However, the footvalve of the engine pump was giving trouble again. I had done a job on it in Tenerife, using steel bolts in its bronze casing. I knew these would not last forever but when we stripped it we found them to be corroded through already. We replaced them with more steel bolts, as that was all we had.

The lack of consistent good wind convinced me that we had nothing to lose by cutting the 'corner' and heading directly for Bermuda, now about seven hundred miles away. We had diesel for about two hundred and fifty miles at this stage.

Sean felt that we had time in hand and that, Bermuda being very expensive, we should be conserving the diesel. There was no particular reason to get there in a hurry. I was for the fastest

102

possible combination of sailing and motoring. There was an element of risk in using diesel, if we could move at all under sail, in that we might need it more later if the wind should fall to nothing at all.

Sean cut my hair. I had asked him to do a job on it that would reduce maintenance. He certainly did.

The grapefruit was now running low. Kevin suggested that Sean consider this and let us have his verdict. Solomon-like, he pronounced that rationing be effected, a half-grapefruit per man per day. That was fine by us. The important thing was to know where you stood.

Danny was nearly hauled overboard in the night. He was having a sleep on the foredeck in the calico jib; I had known about this but when changing watch forgotten to tell anyone. The lads decided to raise the calico jib and hauled away, pulling Danny up and nearly over the side with it! Luckily his harness was clipped on.

Sunday June 1st brought a school of dolphins and a job of sail repairing. But the major social event was Colm's birthday, celebrated with a cake which was a masterpiece, considering the ingredients available. Its base was the soda bread mix, naturally. The flavouring was pineapple, enriched with raisins and Mars bar. Was there a drop of poteen in it too? And this was done in secret so that Colm got a surprise when it was produced after dinner. We adorned it with a big wax candle.

By 28 degrees north the winds were no flukier than they had been a few days earlier at 25° north, so we didn't appear to be losing anything so far, by cutting the corner.

I now have navigation on the brain. I spent a lot of time to-day sighting and plotting, checking the compass and so on. Bermuda is only twenty miles long and very flat so we wouldn't have to be far out to miss it.

We felt sufficiently on top of the crossing to relax somewhat our freshwater ration. Even when clothes are washed and rinsed in fresh water, by the time they are dried the salt in the air gets into them again. And when they are salty they never feel dry. And they are stiff. We shouldn't complain. I have heard stories that the real long-distance heavies rinse their clothes in salt water to get rid of the accumulated salt deposits!

Monday and Tuesday were good days. The wind blew well for us. The Sargasso weed was gone and hardly had Kevin put the line in but a big dolphinfish took the bait. Even our position plots looked credible. We moved the cabin clock back an hour.

Our radio contact with Ireland was weaker but a Boston station, Mike 'CPJ' Mulcahy, was coming in clearly, doing linkman. The forecast gave 'no tropical warnings'. Thanks for reminding us. It was 3 June and we were into the official hurricane season.

The months June to November are the season of tropical storms and hurricanes. All timings of small boat crossings of the Atlantic are set to avoid the possibility of being in the wrong place at the wrong time. These storms are born along the line of ocean from the Cape Verde to the Caribbean. They generally pass north-eastward between Bermuda and the United States. The very biggest vessels have been overwhelmed. A small vessel caught within one hundred miles of the 'eye' would stand little chance of survival.

In our planning we had considered carefully whether to be at sea in the Bermuda area during the month of June was an acceptable risk. The Irish Met. Office had been particularly helpful but were naturally not about to stick their necks out in this matter.

As always, you could do virtually what you liked with the figures. The US Pilot Chart showed that in June, there had been a hurricane in the area in every third year. On the other hand, the statistical probability figures were fractions of percentage points. Taking the broader view, a yacht race from Newport to Bermuda is held every second year in the month of June. We gathered all the information on hurricane warnings; purple sunsets, departure of sea birds and so on. We carefully marked the 'what to do' instructions in the tropical sailing directions and sailed.

On Wednesday the sky went grey and the wind went ahead.

This was all we needed, head winds. We hardened in our sheets for the first time since forever and heeled as we beat towards the north-west. Four hundred miles to go.

Just before dark on Wednesday a shout from the cockpit brought us all out. 'Whales beside us'.

They were all about, jumping and spouting, about fifteen or eighteen of them, 25 or 30 feet long, greeny-black in colour. You could smell their breath, a foul stale smell. Unfortunately, or fortunately, they went astern very quickly and they were only dots a half-mile away when the cameras were ready to go.

We were managing to lay our course close-hauled and make reasonable speed but as soon as the sea built up we would be slowed down.

Midnight Wednesday, 290 miles to go. Wind fallen and engine on. Showers and lightning. Oilskins dragged out of storage. We motored all night into a fresh clear and sunny Thursday.

We tried to sail but after two hours had managed only three miles and that 20 degrees off course. Engine on again. On Thursday night the wind filled in from the north-east and all sail went up. The force 4 became 5 and lifted to force 6. We were in no mind to reef and pressed on overcanvassed determined to extract every last mile from it. A north-bound vessel, *Orange Blossom*, carrying orange concentrate from Santos, Brazil to New York, confirmed our position. Our watch distances were 25 miles plus.

All day Thursday and Friday the wind held up respectably well. We hove-to once to go swimming, and also caught another dolphinfish. Kevin used its head as bait and half an hour later found that the head had been savagely eaten. No one was keen to go swimming again. On Friday afternoon our small transistor radio picked up Radio Bermuda ahead. We were in business.

At 3 a.m. on Saturday the boat was like a boarding school the day before going home. All were awake and about. At 5.15 a.m. we saw it — a light flashing on the horizon ahead. Three thousand miles out of Tenerife, Bermuda was in sight.

105

Approaching Bermuda, Kevin decided that the bearded look was not for him. He is about to shave.

On our 26th day out of Tenerife, Bermuda appeared ahead.

CHAPTER SEVEN

Bermuda

ON OUR twenty-sixth day at sea, we approached the island of Bermuda. The low line on the horizon developed shades, shapes and as we came closer, houses. Not too close, because dangerous reefs front the east side from which we were approaching.

We had the detailed Bermuda chart out now and very quickly, it seemed, the buoys marking the narrow entrance to St. George went past. We rounded close-hauled into the cut, about 150 feet wide. We lost the wind in the shelter of the channel. Luckily, the flooding tide kept us moving inward. The wind caught the top of the mainsail, and then all sails as we heeled and reached across the harbour towards the town.

'This is Bermuda Harbour Radio, *Saint Patrick*. Welcome to Bermuda', came the British accent over the VHF. 'If you tie-up at the wooden jetty on the west side of Ordinance Island ahead of you we'll see if we can get you through Customs as quick as we can.' We sailed past anchored yachts, downed foresail, jib and main and at 12.15 tied alongside.

The black customs man was pleasant and helpful. We had had mixed reports on the attitude of the blacks here to whites so this was a good beginning. He suggested we go round to Somers Wharf where we could tie alongside at no charge. This we did and then in our different ways proceeded to investigate the place. I sat on the jetty wall, taking in the scene and talking to passers-by. The lads disappeared into the town. Yes, a bottle of beer really was two dollars twenty-five. As strollers passed, some stopping and looking at the Hooker, I heard about tropical storm 'Andrew'. This was the first of the 'season' and had been 'born' the previous day. Right now it was causing havoc as it ran up the coast of Carolina. But it wouldn't be bothering Bermuda.

Kevin succeeded in cashing a traveller's cheque — this was a Saturday. While he was away I phoned home, 'collect', as they say, and was in full flight when the operator came back. 'You can't call the Republic of Ireland collect', she said. 'Ah, you can surely', said I. 'Aren't we at it?'. 'No, we can't charge Ireland', she said, and I was cut off. That was a pity, but the main message had got through, and for zero, a lot cheaper than the eleven dollars it cost Sean.

We spent a couple of days in St. George, meeting people, visiting yachts, drinking beer (slowly) and our own wine less slowly. Tom and Helen Gallagher introduced us to the high side of life in Bermuda, in what was to be one of many generous occasions, typical of the people we met there. They had been expecting us and everything was arranged so that we could stay in various houses and take a break from the confines of the *Saint Patrick*. Mary Barry, Suzanne Cronin and Mags Wyer, Johnny's fiancée, were due to fly out on Tuesday night.

On Tuesday we sailed the fifteen miles or so to Hamilton, the capital, motoring at first past a lifting road bridge, blue waters, sandy beaches and tree-lined coves with moored boats. Then we were out into the open sea and sailing on the west side of the island, which really isn't open at all because reefs abound for miles out to the west and you run the risk of stranding on coral if you depart from the marked channels. Ireland Island, three miles or so on the west side, is named, not after our place, but after a 'Mister' Ireland.

Bermuda was to be a staging point for several of the Tall Ships bound for New York from Europe. Bermuda's Department of Tourism had invited us to stop here, so we had accepted, seeing as how we had planned to stop here anyway.

When we got to Hamilton I changed into clean shorts and tee-shirt, oilskin jacket and rubber boots; it was raining cats and dogs. We were assured that it was the first rain for a month and in any event that it wouldn't last long.

In an air-conditioned office I met my man from the Ministry, a jovial black guy. 'What action or activity is planned for the Tall Ships or ourselves?'

The answer was long and sounded good but what it added up to was that we could tie up free of charge and get our garbage collected. 'Thanks a lot', says I to myself.

There was, in fairness to them, to be a high grade barbeque for officers of tall ships and local dignitaries, five hundred in total, but we planned on leaving before it.

On Tuesday evening we met our other hosts, Joe and Jeanne Wakefield, Elizabeth Jones and the Meades, Barry and Brenda. To all, a collective thank-you — and our invitations to Ireland, given in alcohol though they were, are real.

A day or two later the Bermuda newspapers began to carry reports of problems aboard the Norwegian square-rigger, *Christian Radich*. She was about three hundred miles south-east of Bermuda, following more or less the course we had taken. The word was that one of her cadets had died on board from meningitis and there was a question of whether this could spread through her crew.

As it turned out the death of the cadet was an isolated case. The Norwegians did have a doctor on board but their medical supplies were low. The US Air Force, from their Kindley base in Bermuda, helicoptered out supplies of penicillin so that everyone aboard, ninety-seven of them, got a course of shots. By the time they made into St George the fuss was over and the ship didn't have to go into quarantine, as had been proposed.

The American *Barquentine Eagle* is the flagship of the US Coastguard. A magnificent vessel, she was to lead the Parade of Sail in New York on the Fourth of July. She was now anchored in Hamilton Roads and appeared to be a hive of activity. A continual traffic of mini-coastguard boats ferried to

109

and from the shore. Activity on her deck appeared to be continuous: flags flew by day, lights by night.

We radioed her.

'Captain Barry presents his compliments to your Captain and invites him to drinks aboard the Irish sailing cutter *Saint Patrick*, 18.00 hours. Saturday. Over'.

A long silence followed as a cadet radio officer wrestled with this protocol-ridden proposition.

'Your message is acknowledged and will be relayed. However, the Captain is not presently aboard and it is thought that he may have other plans. Over.'

'Very good. I'll convey that to Captain Barry', says I. 'Thank you and out'.

'U.S. *Eagle* to *Saint Patrick*. Acknowledged and out'.

Well, our crowd thought this was hilarious cheek but I thought it a very reasonable thing to do.

Afterwards, the sailing master of the *Eagle* came, 'Red' Shannon. He would have called on us anyway, as he had seen us about. He knew Connemara well, having spent summers there as a boy, and was familiar with the Hookers.

The following morning we went aboard the *Eagle* at Red's invitation and she was a sight to see. The United States had acquired her as a prize of war from Germany in 1945; she had been a German naval training ship before the war. Red had asked the day before whether there was anything we needed. We told him. 'Well, I can't do anything about money!' Red said. 'I may be able to organise some diesel, and we'd be delighted to present you with a US flag'.

'And that shroud', he said pointing to our repaired port shroud, 'let us make you a new one'.

True to his word he got his riggers to make an exact copy of our damaged one, and he presented us with a stars and stripes. Unfortunately he found he couldn't do anything on the diesel because, being a US vessel in British waters, they had to account to Her Majesty's Customs in Bermuda for all diesel used.

On board *Eagle* there were a lot of youngsters on anchor

110

watch, boarding ladder watch, radio watch and so on, in other words a lot of standing around. To my mind there should have been some sailing going on, say a half-dozen skiffs where the cadets would get a close up 'hands-on' feel for the wind and sea and boat handling under sail. As it was we were told that the *Eagle* motors mostly, doing very little sailing.

The *Christian Radich* was a different kettle of fish. Her sails and running rigging have a well-used look about them. We were aboard her as a guest of the bosun, Chris, who is from Belfast, of all places. He is married to a Norwegian girl and when work ran thin at home emigrated to Norway. Chris told us that, although their ship was government run, funds were mighty tight and they tried to supplement them wherever possible by selling off bits and pieces of old sails, belaying pins, anything. He reckoned they sailed to save on diesel. But looking around at the lively youngsters and the cut of their officers, Chris included, I reckoned that they simply loved to sail their ship.

And then there were the yachts in from the Newport-Bermuda Race. Eight of these were in the 'Maxi' class, 80-foot racing machines. We were sitting on the deck of the *Patrick* when the first of these, *Condor*, came in, creaming across the harbour, spinnaker flying, with her crew of twenty-six on deck. Next was *Nirvana*, holder of the record for the Fastnet Race. One of her crew was Neil O hUadhaigh, whose family live just round the corner from Sean and myself in Monkstown. Neil is one of *Nirvana's* half-dozen professional full-time crew. The other eighteen or so, including the owner, come aboard only at race time.

He asked us to join them the following Friday for a picnic/sail around. I would have loved that, but we had to be away. However Mary, Suzanne and Mags, who were staying awhile, went out and had a very eventful day.

A large crowd went aboard *Nirvana* in relaxed and good humour. The owner and his family, some crew and various friends were there, all in fine form. The conversation flowed.

'See that fellow — he's the skipper, one of the world's top

racing skippers, and we have the best navigator in the world'.

Some time later the helmsman saw rocks ahead.

'Should we not tack?' he asked. No reply.

'Is it not time to go about?' he tried again. No one paid any attention to him. Crash! as the keel struck coral. It was like hitting a wall. All were thrown forward. A man at the bow shot over-board. They were lucky the mast held up.

Unfortunately the atmosphere aboard had been somewhat too relaxed!

All ended well insofar as they got the boat off the rocks, and later went ahead with a very elegant lunch. The owner didn't seem put out at the prospect of a $50,000 repair bill but was very concerned for all his crew and guests. Needless to say, the skipper, understandably upset, was not the 'life and soul' of the party thereafter.

Our own sailing round the Island had been less spectacular. At an early stage, snorkling, I discovered a line wrapped round the propeller shaft — the missing length of our Walker log line. We had crossed the Atlantic with a line fouling the shaft! I tried to hacksaw it, diving with mask and snorkel, but it was iron-hard and even when cut would not come off. I had to get the air bottles on and using a screwdriver and the hacksaw prised about fifteen feet of line off in short lengths.

We were to make our departure from St George, so on Wednesday 18 June we sailed the Hooker from Hamilton. Danny, Sean and myself took her, with Mary along for the sail, and Neil from *Nirvana*. As it happened there was a spanking wind blowing out of a blue sky with some heavy showers. Neil was thrilled with the sail. This time we went through the lifting bridge in Ferry Reach under sail. The wind was strong and dead aft and too late I discovered that the width of the boat and squared-off boom left no room at all for deviation. I'll never forget Mary's look from the hatch as Johnny and Neil hauled on the mainsheet as the boom scraped by the bridge pier. To tell the truth we probably had a couple of feet to spare, but at five or six knots it didn't feel like it.

The night before we left, the weather people at Kindley Air

Base gave us a detailed forecast. It wasn't terrific at all. There would be head winds in a couple of days but the wind forces expected were not high so there was no reason not to go. They gave us the position and speed of the 'Gulf Stream' and were about to give details of some 'cold eddies' which might be useful when I stopped them and explained that as we weren't using Satellite Navigation we would be in no position to benefit by such precise information.

I am not at all against such electronic equipment. It's terrific and whenever/if ever I can afford it, I will get it. However, I see too much dependence on it. The day before we left St George we met an Italian yacht, about 45-foot long, a fine boat, bound for Europe by way of the Azores. She had been waiting ten days for some parts needed for her 'Sat. Nav.' She had a sextant (she had everything). But they weren't keen to depend on it. I find that sort of upside-down thinking extraordinary, but dependence on electronics is becoming the norm.

Our time was up. We had already stretched an extra day into our time here. We slept on the boat on Wednesday, 18 June; tomorrow we would leave at first light.

These are dangerous waters. Only a couple of years earlier the *Marques,* a sail training ship, had been lost, while on a race from Bermuda to Halifax. However in this case, it is felt in some quarters that poor ship's management contributed to the loss. The matter is presently before the US Courts.

The alarm in the *Patrick* went off at 6 a.m., and could hardly be heard for the rain pelting on the deck. The wind blew through our rigging and that of the two big Baltic Traders outside of which we were tied. There was no sense in getting up to that so it was back to sleep for an hour.

When daylight came it was only to allow the rain, blowing near horizontally, to be seen. However, it was only a passing shower of the tropical type, and by 8 a.m. we were sailing out of the harbour, with all reefs in the mainsail.

There are two beacons guarding the northern approach to Bermuda, both of which should be left to port before laying off to the United States. We were half-way to the far beacon when

113

Two days out of Bermuda, a north-easterly gale forced us to the west. That gale put us 90 miles off course.

I realised we had gone well inside the first one and were now in the very waters that they protected. What to do? The chart showed a maze of shallows but as far as I could see few that would threaten our six foot draft. The tidal rise here, a couple of feet, was of little consequence. From where we were, it seemed that it was no safer to go towards one beacon than the other. So for the far one we made, and I was the relieved navigator when we reached it. A stranding here would have been entirely due to my carelessness. What had happened was that the first mark we sighted was the far one. Even though it was fifteen degrees inside the expected course, I had said to go for it, because none other was in sight at the time. An inexcusable laxity.

That day, the Thursday, is best forgotten. In between torrential rain showers, the wind varied from virtually nothing at all to strong squalls in which we had to down all sail and run before it. Not a ray of sunshine relieved the gloom. From the log I see that, in a five-hour period, we were full-reefed, half-reefed, full-reefed again before a squall. We knocked out a reef, all reefs and shortly pulled down all sail in more squalls. All the while the damp penetrated our clothes and bunks.

By the early hours of Friday, things were much better. The sky had cleared, the moon was up and we were close hauled to a steady force 4 from the north-east. Even at two in the morning the little matter of paper clogging the pump intake was cheerfully dealt with. We thought that it must have been the complete works of Shakespeare that went into the bilges, because for days we were clearing the pump-well of paper. It was in fact only one paperback, that had fallen down behind a bunk.

During Friday the wind veered to the south-east to give us perfect sailing with the wind on our quarter. We changed up to the big jib and clothes were hung out to dry. Breakfasts 'go leór' were consumed as the miles flew by. The five-day forecast from Kindley Air Base, with two days of moderate head winds in the offing, was far from our minds. By 6 p.m. on Friday a hundred and sixty miles lay astern between ourselves and Bermuda.

Occasionally we would bring a bucket of water in over the

side to check the sea temperature, consistently running at 23 degrees. A rise in temperature would be the essential indicator of the presence of the gulf stream, which flows in a north-east direction at about $2\frac{3}{4}$ knots. Like a river in the ocean, its width in this area is about fifty miles.

An afternoon position plot put our distance to Boston at 540 miles. The wind went to the south-west and we gybed, and later went further to the westward and freshened. Somewhat overpressed, we doused the foresail and sailed on reefed main and jib.

The weather forecasts were by now speaking of a deepening low centred at 39 north, 64 west by Saturday p.m. This was the weather system that was to bring us the moderate head-winds. However the emphasis now placed on it indicated that stronger winds were likely.

Saturday, 2 a.m. Electrical storm off to the east. Cloudy for us. Beam wind. Warm and pleasant. Log 212 (adjusted + 6%). Barometer 1005.

Then follows an entry scribbled in a wet and hasty hand.

Big squall, plus rain.
Ran before it and downed foresail. Water into cabin.

From then until the dawn the conditions were joyless. The wind veered to the north-west, forcing us to close-haul to the east of our course. The morning was grey and wet. A persistent light rain fell, the wind backed to the south-west and became light and fitful.

By mid-afternoon the wind, such as it was, was moved round to the north-east. 'Good — that means the front is passing', said I, adding 'I think'.

A quarter of an hour later another squall, also from the north-east raised an extraordinary amount of white caps on the water. On a hunch we took the sea-water temperature and found it to be up 2 degrees. We were now in the gulf stream, two hundred and eighty miles north of Bermuda.

That squall from the north-east never let up. We took down the mainsail and bore-away towards the north-west, sailing with only the jib. The seas, choppy earlier on, began to build-up as the wind blew over the current.

Sunday 2 a.m. log 320 miles. Still very wet going!
6 a.m. Big seas. Close to breaking.
10 a.m. Strong wind, certainly force 8, maybe 9. Huge breaking seas. Pumping regularly.

The danger now was that one of these breaking seas might catch us abeam and throw us over. However we were making 3 or 4 knots and on the occasions so far when a white breaker was coming down on us we had managed to slew the Hooker's starboard quarter round towards it. The crest would run beneath us as we momentarily surfed towards Carolina, or thereabouts.

As it was we were able to make progress not too far west of where we wanted to go. And there was a fair possibility the push of the gulf stream would actually compensate and keep us on line.

That was all theory and of little interest. No cooking or eating had taken place all day. Immediately your on-deck watch was over it would be straight into a bunk, oilskins and all. Soup and tea were slopped up, spilling and scalding over wet and numb hands. Bloody miserable, but we were getting along.

Getting along where was, of course, the question. We hadn't had a position for two days, but we weren't worried on that score as there was sea-room in plenty. We must by now have been out of the gulf stream again. No one felt like going through the exercise of taking the sea temperature. In bad weather even the simplest jobs can take on mammoth proportions.

During the later part of Sunday, patches of blue appeared through the clouds. The wind fell to force seven or so, or at least it seemed to. Maybe it was the bit of sun made it appear to ease. But no, there was a definite reduction in the level of noise, both from the sea and from the wind. Earlier they had been indistinguishable from one another. Now the whine of the wind was a distinct entity from the crashing and rushing of the wave tops.

By 10 p.m. on Sunday the worst was over. Log entries were being made again. A tuna goulash was boiled up and devoured. There was even some conversation — mostly about where we might now be! Tomorrow we could possibly even see some vessels on the north Atlantic shipping lanes.

By two a.m. on Monday a big moon shone over the heaving seas, now much reduced. The air was chilly. So were we. And tired and wet. Wonder of wonders, we started to get American radio stations crackling in.

The wind backed north and eased and we lay off further, to the west by north-west, without complaining. We got the mainsail up again fully reefed. Our lack of comment on the un-favourable wind direction was rewarded some hours later by a wind change to the west — force 5 or so we estimated, as we could let out one reef. We could now, for the first time in days, sail our course — due north magnetic.

At 4.30 a.m. Sean said 'You can smell the sweet hay on the warm west breeze'. As we were a couple of hundred miles at least from any field, hayfield or otherwise, I thought Sean's sense of smell was over-perceptive.

At eight in the morning saw a VTOO (Visitor To Our Ocean). Nasty weather is back with us again. From the south-west, lumpy seas and grey skies. However, not nearly as bad as a few days ago. The peak halyard has come loose and out of a block and we had to drop the mainsail.

It wasn't until half-eleven that we got the halyard re-reeved and the mainsail up again, blessed relief. In deference to our ragged condition we still had a reef in, even though the wind, now force four south-west, hardly warranted it.

Our distance run tallied, but we were way in to the west,

119

On a fine evening we sometimes struck up music; guitar, button accordian, uileann pipes, spoons and bodhrán.

The fuel tank was taken out and cleaned.

about ninety miles off our course for Nantucket. It's easy to rationalise this afterwards — the gulf stream being only 50 miles wide, cold eddies, leeway on our north-west heading and so on. It did settle one thing, on which I had doubts anyway. We would go for Boston not outside of the Nantucket Shoals and Cape Cod, but by the inside route through the Cape Cod Canal. Our location was 150 miles from the islands of New England. We were now close enough to use a chart of the United States East Coast. On this we plotted our position and lay off our course, adjusting the grid on the steering compass to suit — satisfied men now that we knew where we were and where we were going.

About this time the engine coughed and died. (We made a point of running it now and again). It sounded like fuel starvation. Sure enough the filter was full of water and muck stirred up from the fuel tank. We installed a direct feed to the engine from one of our spare fuel drums, changed the filter and got the engine going. 'Ready for service', as they say in the life-boat journal.

On this Monday night we had our first proper dinner for three days. Kevin wrote:

Excellent. Crew's spirits restored (but still damp). Fine sailing conditions. We have all changed into our dryest wet clothes, a welcome change from the salty, sweaty garb... the radar reflector is now up.

We judged that we were bound to meet the European shipping lanes into New York shortly and that in the heavy traffic it would be as well to be seen.

Even though the sailing conditions were better, with a steady beam wind, the fatigue still carried on. The sleeping bags were still sodden, and it was colder, so sleep was not easy. I would say no-one, except Sean, was sleeping. It was more of a dozing in the sauna-like cocoon of your bag as the heated damp eventually warmed.

About two a.m. on Tuesday, just as I had squeezed into my

121

bag, Danny gave me a shout. 'Paddy, the topping lift is broken'. 'Let it be until morning', I said. Hopefully we would not have to reef in the meantime.

At 7 a.m. the sun was up and the day was looking good, if chilly. A US Coastguard Cutter, *Point Franklin*, approached to within a hundred yards and called on the radio to us to identify ourselves. 'Galway Hooker *Saint Patrick*. Bound from Ireland to New York for the Statue of Liberty Sail-Past', we told them. They seemed satisfied with that. We hardly looked like anyone's first choice as high-speed drug-smuggling transport!

'Could you give us a weather forecast and position?', we asked. Incredibly, they said they couldn't. I suppose they didn't want to disclose their position on the air in case 'baddies' might hear it. But what was to stop them coming over and talking directly to us? However, in fairness, they did contact Mike Mulcahy in Boston for us. We had had difficulty getting through to him on the short-wave radio. Unfortunately, Mike got the impression that we were not in great shape, sails torn and boat drifting. This, of course, was patently untrue, otherwise the coastguard would hardly have left us. What was in poor order was our VHF, and this may have given the impression that we were beat-up in a general way.

The morning brought a light sailing wind and haze with visibility just enough to get a sight. We were, inexplicably, thirty-five miles to the west and ten miles short of our estimated position. A new course was laid off towards Buzzards Bay, eighty-five miles away.

We baked bread. The wind rose to about force six and I brought forward our estimated sighting of land. By seven, spray and waves were coming over the side occasionally. We were dressed in our long trousers, woolly socks, boots, the lot. How quickly the shorts and tee-shirt weather and the flying fish had been left behind.

We had to be in Boston on Friday at noon. Checking out distances it looked as if we had about a day in hand. Up ahead we had a choice of places: Newport (we would probably be there later); Block Island (very crowded, I had heard); New Bedford,

122

the official port of entry, without attraction, as far as we knew; Nantucket has fog one day in two at this time of year and if we got fog-bound we could be late for Boston; Martha's Vineyard, perfect in every respect, we reckoned.

As the wind rose further we dropped the foresail at dusk. Barely had the darkness fallen than ahead of our port bow flashed the green light of Block Island. America in sight!

CHAPTER EIGHT

American Welcome

A FERRY boat carrying early commuters to the mainland gave us a hoot as we gybed round into Vineyard Haven and sailed in to the mooring and docking area. We put our stars and stripes from *Eagle* on our shroud and the Tricolour on our stern. Sandy beaches and an assortment of wooden buildings and timber jetties edged a bay where a mixed selection of interesting well-used sailing boats were anchored. There was a beautiful stillness in the crisp sunny morning air. Several yachts had people break-fasting on deck. 'They all look like Kennedys,' said Kevin.

By 8.30 the boat was tied up and all of us sitting down ashore in that great American institution, the 'diner'. We consumed a mountain of real United States breakfast and coffee, coffee and more coffee as we stretched our bones. The harbour-master was starting his day a couple of tables down. He was very insistent that we clear customs, but yes, it could wait until we had eaten.

The *Vineyard Gazette* had a reporter down to us even as we were still drinking coffee. News sure travels fast in this place. Mark, the reporter, told us that some of the Newport boats returning after the race had turned back to Bermuda because of the gale. This made us feel a lot better.

Colm went to work on cleaning out our diesel tank and I to the matter of customs. Dan and Kyra West owned and operated 'our' jetty and boatyard. Dan was related to the

Eldridge of the yellow Eldridge Tide and Pilot book. His grand-
father had written it. When Dan saw that we were operating on
a two-year-old copy of the book, with pencilled adjustments for
the difference in moon phase, he presented us with a 1986
version — from which I saw that my attempts to correct the
out-of-date issue were mathematically weak — wrong,
actually.

The US Customs wanted us to go to the official port of entry of
New Bedford, twenty miles back — and they were very
keen. The Department of Immigration and Agriculture would
also want to see us. After hours on the phone, Kyra succeeded
in charming a first-class solution — we would clear
immediately on arriving in Boston on next Friday. That was a
fair old trick, considering that Boston was about ninety miles
distant through US coastal waters and two days hence.

The town of Oak Bluffs is about four miles away and it was
to there we repaired that evening. We had been asked to come
to the 'Ocean View' and to bring the music. The bar was too
crowded and the baseball on the TV too loud for much music so
we had plenty of beer instead, very little of which we had to pay
for. And we all got tee-shirts — Danny produced them. He said
that a fellow behind the bar gave them to him for us. We taxi'd
back, with the money we'd saved on beer, to sleep the sleep of
the dead until the alarm shrilled at six.

Such an early call was not by choice, but by virtue of the
necessity to beat the turn of the tide in the narrow passage we
would take through the islands near Woods Hole. Woods Hole
is the oceanographic centre from where the *Titanic* discovery
and survey was organised. Kyra had worked there as a Russian
interpreter. There is apparently a good deal of co-operation
between Americans and Russians in the field of oceanography,
with regular joint ventures. Going out into Buzzards Bay on a
sunny morning, with the haze making the shore on either side
fairly devoid of marks, we raised sail for the ten miles or so to
the entrance of this canal.

I was unprepared for the size of it and for the green un-
blemished countryside around. I think of canals in the context

of Dublin's Grand Canal and its associated hinterland. The Cape Cod Canal is wide and deep so as to take ocean-going vessels. It is managed by the Army Corps of Engineers. Its overhead bridges are high and long. Sailing in the canal is not allowed — a pity, because we had a following wind.

An easy drift up the sandy shore of Massachusetts brought us to the approximate location of Scituate. There we planned to call in for the night. Only where was it? In the easy atmosphere of the afternoon rigorous navigation, indeed any navigation, was let lie — apart from keeping off the shore, that is. Now we had the embarrassment of having to enquire 'Where is Scituate?' We approached a small motor boat, fishing. Just as we got to within hailing distance she upped and offed. We sailed toward another speed-boat, waving them over to us. They waved back and they too shot off. We finally got a fellow to talk to us. He seemed surprised that such a weathered bunch as we must have looked did not know where Scituate was. 'Why, right in there', he said, pointing out a breakwater a quarter mile back, busy with boats going in and out.

Humbly, we dropped sail and engined into this busy entrance with motor boats and sail boats under power, at least six of them, within forty yards of us. You'd sure want to know the 'rules of the road' around here. As it was, the colour of marker buoys, green to port and red to starboard, was the opposite of what we were used to.

Inside, a huge expanse of water opened out, the size of Dun Laoghaire Harbour but with boats in every square yard of it. We mooched along the right-hand side of the channel, as slowly as we could. The harbour-master, relaxed and puffing his pipe, motored up.

'Any hope we could go alongside?', we asked.

He pointed to some fishing boats tied up to a partly-completed wharf.

'That'll do us grand', we thanked him. We looked at the names of some of the fishing boats — *Irish Piper*, *Irish Mist*. We were getting close to Boston.

Round the cabin table we sat, the six of us, having a rum before bed.

With music playing we sailed into Boston harbour.

'I suppose there'll be speeches to-morrow', someone said.
'So what?'

'We'll have to get our speech ready, Ha, Ha, Ha.'

I suppose it was the rum talking, but until the early hours we made speeches to each other, speeches of welcome, speeches of history, speeches of immigration, speeches to the Department of Immigration. We laughed and laughed and the crack was mighty. We finished the bottle of rum; next thing the alarm seemed to be ringing.

A partial turnout of crew mustered on deck as we cleared the harbour at eight in the morning. I went back to bed: 'Wake me when we get to the Graves Island Light off Boston'.

The chart of Boston Harbour shows a maze of islands, rocks and shoals protecting the bay within, almost as complex as the shores of south Connemara. We were, at 11.30, moving slowly in a light breeze inwards through the North Channel. 'Off Castle Island at 12' was our arrangement. I had a job finding that on the chart at all because it has a castle all right but hasn't been an island for many a long year.

As Castle Island came closer we could see a boat approaching with'POLICE' marked in large letters on its side. As it closed we could see that there were a lot of people aboard — a very large number indeed, all cheering and waving and cameras.

'Fáilte go Boston' came over the police boat loud-hailer. We had come to the right place all right.

Out came two tugs, hooters deafening us, and then a couple of red fire boats, hosing into the sky. 'Up Rosmuc' read the banner on one most peculiar-looking motorised 'pedalo'. Colm was talking Irish to them as the tins of beer came at us like leaves off a tree on a breezy autumn day. Sean took the helm as we struck up our music, sailing in towards Charlestown. 'Pay no attention to my antics when we land', said Colm, pulling out a *báinín* coat and putting it on. A crowd on Pier 4 waved and shouted as we dropped sail and pulled alongside. Before we touched, Colm gave a mighty leap. Now we knew what he was on about. Hugs and handshakes and kisses — it was hard to get the boat tied up with it all. Wives, relations, strangers, friends, newspapers and TV were there, relations of the Caseys who built the Hooker, the Conroys who owned her, Tom 'Bottle' who sailed her long ago, Colm's sister Maura, who had done so much work for us in Boston with the dance and all; meeting and talking and being introduced and photographed. Old people, some who hadn't seen Connemara this sixty years, stood silently by, tears running down their creased faces. A strong handshake, a quick soft 'cómhgáirdeachas' — no words could describe what seeing *Bád Chonroí* again meant to these people.

There was to be an official reception later and a dance in Savin Hill Yacht Club for us tomorrow. Anne Reilly had done a most elegant job of organising a reception with the best of food and drink laid on in abundance. The Irish Ambassador came up from Washington and said some nice things. The Governor of Massachusetts and the Mayor of Boston had Parchments and Proclamations read.

'WHEREAS Man's conquest of the sea has spread knowledge and civilisation throughout the world; and
WHEREAS The settlement and development of the Commonwealth of Massachusetts was made possible by the pioneer immigrants and settlers to our shores: and
WHEREAS The rich maritime history of the Commonwealth of Massachusetts is a testimony to the valiant seamen who opened the sea-lanes of international trade and commerce and foreign ports, and
WHEREAS The intrepid sailors of *Saint Patrick* of Galway, Ireland have enriched the lore of the sea with their skill, courage and seamanship in sailing their proud craft from Ireland to Boston, Massachusetts
NOW THEREFORE I Michael S. Dukakis, Governor of the Commonwealth of Massachusetts do hereby proclaim June 27, 1986 as

IRISH SAILORS' DAY.

Was this for real?

Two happy men, Danny and Colm.

With a mighty jump he arrived in America!

I stepped forward to reply and, peculiar as it may seem, words came easily. I thanked Anne and Ray Reilly and Maura who had done so much, my own sister Síle de Barra, Ann Dougherty and Ann Graham, John Curran of the Voice of Erin radio station, Mike Mulcahy, Colm and Brigid O'Riordan who had given us the use of their house and had actually had a heavy mushroom mooring anchor laid for us out in Nantucket Island. I then spoke freely and briefly (I hope) of the Hooker, our voyage and our appreciation of the reception. And anyone who wanted a sail was very welcome.

But my mind was wandering ahead. The fund-raising/ sponsorship efforts had not produced anything like the amount needed. Even with the $6,000 we would be getting for taking a group aboard on the Fourth of July on the Liberty Parade, we were in poor financial shape.

I'll tell you it was hard to get a night's sleep in that town. The next day we sailed, about thirty of us, to Savin Hill with three *currachaí adhmaid* pulling beside us — great to see. There was little wind so the lads rowing didn't have much trouble keeping ahead. That night was mighty. Dancing and singing and drinking — beer and whiskey together — you couldn't say no, and *Saint Patrick* tee-shirts on half the hall by now. That céilí paid our air-fares home. But more important by far was what Louis Hughes and Jim Murphy quietly said to me: 'Paddy, we know ye have a problem with shipping the Hooker home. P. J. Carroll would like to pay the cost of getting her back'.

Well, if I was wearing a hat I would have thrown it in the air. I was dumbfounded. Here, at two in the morning, was the best news, the finest present we could have had. 'Can I tell the others?' 'Sure — now go and enjoy yourself,' said Jim, 'we'll see you tomorrow for a meal'. I slept content that night.

Somewhere along the way we lost contact with Danny. Occasional sightings indicated that he was alive and well in South Boston. He sent word that he would see us in New York.

Unfortunately, we had to be away from Boston by midnight on that Sunday because the Mayor of Newport was keen that we be there on Monday evening for a party. Always willing, though weakening, we mustered at Savin Hill and put out to sea through Boston Harbour. It was a hundred miles to Newport, but favourable tides shortened that.

This was a great opportunity to catch up on sleep and it seemed that before we knew it we were at Brenton Reef Tower off Newport, having engined all the way. We naturally put up sail for going into Newport and obligingly the afternoon south-wester let us cut a dash as we swept past the millionaires' mansions and lawns to tie up at Christie's dock.

Pat Horgan, Mayor Pat Kirby and Newport A.O.H. put on a great welcome with eats, drinks and a generous spontaneous whip-around. We sold *Saint Patrick* tee-shirts in between.

Some of the Tall Ships bound for New York were here and there was to be a Parade of Sail on the Tuesday. Our preparation for this international event took the form of entertaining the crew of the French sailing barque, *Belem*, on the Hooker. From later accounts the schooner *Spirit of Massachusetts* was also ably represented — music and drinking — was there to be no end to it?

Pat Horgan of Christie's put on a breakfast that put the life back into us as, with a goodly load of passengers, we set out for the Parade. A bright sun lit the bay as the chilly breeze barely filled the sails, Most boats used motor to get into place as the Parade moved off. We were to have been in the group following the Portuguese square-rigger, the 300-foot *Sagres*, but we could see only spectator boats and confusion behind her so we lined in ahead instead. The coastguard boats fairly successfully kept the channel clear of spectator boats. Persistent offenders were hosed — it seemed very effective.

Our participant status was not known to all the coastguard vessels, apparently: a loud-hailer yelled, 'Black sailboat, get off the Parade fairway. Turn right'. The answer they got reddened their ears! Fair play to them, they apologised immediately when they found us on the printed parade list. Many of the spectator boats, sixty- and eighty-footers, were bigger than us.

The wind came up as it does here on summer afternoons, and soon we were flying with sails squared out. The parade channel

JIM DAVIS   BOSTON HERALD

This says it all!

narrowed as some fools in spectator boats dodged about, kamikaze-like. We had to start our engine and put it full astern at one stage, to avoid chopping an expensive motor yacht in two. The coastguard appeared to be gone for their tea as chaos abounded. We got up on to the weather-side of *Cuauhtemoc*, the big Mexican three-master, and stayed close by her. This did the job.

But what was it going to be like in New York?

The *Captain's Handbook* for Opsail 1986 measures two inches in thickness. Every minute detail covering the movement and organisation of the two hundred and fifty ships in the parade seemed to be covered. The sail past the Statue of Liberty for her centennial was to be an impressive event.

Saint Patrick and the Danish ship *Elinor* were to be guests of Riverside, twenty miles outside New York, on Wednesday 2 July. An overnight passage, this time with good sailing all the way, brought us the 105 miles through Long Island sound into the rural ambiance of Riverside. More entertainment, and late to bed.

In the calm of the early morning Long Island Sound had a magical quality. Boats were gliding out from creeks, harbours and coves up and down from us. Five miles across on the Long Island side it was the same. All were turning west for New York, New York. By seven the skyscrapers of Manhattan could be seen on the skyline.

On 3 July all the participating parade boats, except for the very biggest ones, were to meet at the top of the East River at about nine and sail informally down through New York. By the time we got to Throg's Neck bridge the river was awash with boats of all sizes and shapes, parade boats and spectator boats together. This was entirely informal, with an added rule — one-way traffic only. The river banks and bridges were lined with cheering people. With a fresh westerly wind heading us we had some fun tacking diagonally across the fleet. You sure get to know people that way! 'Are you really from Ireland?', they

134

shouted at us as they recognised our Tricolour and the name *Saint Patrick*. We stoked the fire to raise more smoke.

Manhattan Bridge coming up. Could we sail between the pier and the shore? The chart made it look possible, but I funked it. Then Brooklyn Bridge and Wall Street, still waving and shouting and breathless. At Pier 17 three balconies were put to the test as the crowd in a restaurant clapped us by. Then it was away out into lower New York bay, leaving the fun and excitement behind us as we went to our designated berth. It was still early, about twelve noon.

The rest of that day was a disaster. Larry Ottway's group in four currachs gallantly made their way down-river to meet us but the berth in Bay Ridge, for them as for us, was unsuitable — too exposed. We waited for hours for word of an alternative while political 'latchicos' preened and got themselves photographed with us. Eventually, left more or less to fend for ourselves, we made back for South Street Seaport. There we were made to feel decidedly unwelcome.

'Could we even put some of our people ashore?'

'Twenty-five dollars.'

'I'd jump in the river first', I said.

'You can stay the night for $3 a foot', they eventually conceded.

'Ah, go on! Talk to Opsail. They invited us to this city and said it was OK to come in here.'

After further unpleasantries, we did get an overnight berth there. Unfortunately the fare-paying arrangement for passengers on the Fourth of July had fallen through. Late that night I made phone calls to some very surprised and delighted people.

'Would we like to sail in the Parade on the *Saint Patrick*? Are you serious?'

'Sure I am. We have some room. We'd be glad to have you'.

Their effusive thanks put the heart in us somewhat again. We were all in good spirits, about twenty of us, as we headed the following morning to the staging area for the parade. Now

135

We sailed down the East River past Manhattan.

we were going to have to do things by the book, the Opsail *Captain's Handbook*, and this we did.

The twenty-two big ones, those huge fully-rigged sailing ships that could not get under Throg's Neck Bridge, had approached New York from the south and were anchored in Sandy Hook Bay. The other 230 vessels were in Gravesend Bay. There we took shore bearings and anchored in station.

The morning was sunny and warm. You could feel the excitement. Anchored around us were some of the finest sailing ships afloat: *Bluenose II* from Canada, *Ticonderoga, British Soldier, Bounty, Black Jack, Shabab Oman* — famous names were all about us. In the distance of Sandy Hook we could see the great white square-riggers approaching.

Eagle led off, bang on time, to pass under the Verrazano Narrows Bridge at ten o'clock. Two escort vessels, *Spirit of Massachusetts* (our friends) and *Bowdoin* flanked her. A wedge of tugs cleared the way. Coastguard vessels lined the fairway keeping spectator boats back. There were 40,000 spectator boats expected and I would say they all came.

Danmark went by, *Libertad* from Argentina, *Esmeralda* from Chile — there had been controversy about that one; she was allegedly used as a torture ship not so long ago. We recognised most as they appeared, out of parade sequence and with lengthening delays between them. The *Amerigo Vespucci* from Italy we recognised, and *Cuauhtemoc* of Mexico, who had protected us in Newport.

There was something definitely amiss with the parade. Our timing for upping anchor and getting into line was an hour gone. The big boats were running way behind. We got up sail, hauled anchor and eased over to where the US Naval Academy sailboats were anchored. They were to be just ahead of us in the line. They shrugged their shoulders, knowing no more than ourselves. The fleet of Dutch boats, thirty-six of them, cargoed over by a sponsored arrangement, were to be ahead of us in the fleet. We decided to pass the time reaching over and back in Gravesend Bay. There was a fine wind for sailing.

An hour and a half late, but no matter to us, we sailed into

137

station in the line and passed under the Narrows Bridge. We had studied the line-up and were briefed on what boats should be ahead and beside us. Our group consisted of eighteen rows of four boats per row. We were in the tenth row, right-hand side, *Yankee Clipper* ahead of us, *Switzerland* and *Vendredi 13* beside us. *Wang Fee*, a Chinese Junk sailed from Australia, was to be behind us. According to the *Handbook*, the coastguard would assist in getting vessels into correct order.

What actually happened was reminiscent of the Charge of the Light Brigade. The boats were there all right, but anything like rows and lines there were not, and may the devil take the hindmost! We thrived on it, full sail pulling to a following force 5 or so as, close to the gybe, we powered up lower New York harbour. All boats carried sail, though most had their engines running; you could see by the exhausts. The *Kyrenia*, a forty-six footer from Greece, pulled up beside us and we trimmed our sails. Side by side, we sailed towards Manhattan.

Spectator boats lined the way a quarter of a mile deep, big and small. Huge ferries on anchor listed as their crowd watched from the parade side. The *Bounty* was firing cannon shots every now and again. Thomas Lipton's huge J-Class *Shamrock* sailed our way. We passed the Dutch fleet. 'We may be the sailors, but they are better fund-raisers', was remarked.

Now we were approaching the Statue of Liberty and the excitement grew. The Cunard *Queen Elizabeth II*, with eight hundred prize-winning car salesmen and their wives aboard, lay anchored. Immediately opposite Liberty Island, from the aircraft carrier *USS Kennedy* until abeam the World Trade Center, vessels were to render 'passing honours' to the reviewing party, which included Presidents Reagan and Mitterrand, on Governors' Island.

The US Naval Academy boats gunned their motors and succeeded at last in getting into line. Square-riggers manned the yards. Colm, Sean and Mary danced to a reel on our deck while we dipped the peak of our mainsail three times — the Galway Hookers' traditional homage to Saint Macdara. It was great being there in the thick of it and enjoying it. This was a

Lady Liberty seen from Saint Patrick.

party after all. We could see the Irish Navy vessel, *LE Eithne*, anchored on the New Jersey side. We dipped sail and she replied.

The parade over, we berthed on the New Jersey side and commenced to sell on the quayside commemorative plaques showing the Hooker, a consignment of which had come in from Ireland the day before. That wasn't much fun, but we had to try and raise cash somehow.

That evening there was a marvellous fireworks display around Manhattan and the Statue of Liberty.

The traffic in Manhattan later that night was chaos itself, but the good humour of the crowds was extraordinary. We were all to meet in Flanagans Bar, but half of us never made it.

CHAPTER NINE

Finale

SATURDAY 5 July was the first day in almost three months that none of us was aboard the *Saint Patrick*. We put our feet up, read the newspaper accounts of the Fourth and watched TV re-runs of the events.

I met Eamon Doran in his bar/restaurant on 52nd Street. 'Why didn't you let us know before now? We could have organised a welcome, fund-raising, the lot', he said. 'Can you bring the Hooker over to the Manhattan side to-morrow and take out a fare-paying party?'

Could we what!

Next morning we sailed the Hooker across to Pier 83, on the west side, where the Circle line sightseeing boats tie up. Eamon was true to his word, and better. Not only did he bring down a large party but he put us in touch with other Irish bars who each organised outings. Larry Ottway's Currach people gave a party for us.

We could be at it yet, but arrangements to cargo the Hooker home had advanced. There was a ship leaving Newark for Liverpool next Monday that could take her.

And it did. Louis Purton, who all week had helped sail and entertain people round New York Harbour, also sailed with me to Newark. There we joked and chatted with the longshoremen while the Hooker was lifted out and made ready for sea again, this time as deck cargo.

The proposed berth at New York was very exposed. Locally based currachs came out to meet us.

We were all homeward bound.

Stories about the Liberty week-end were legion. Security had been paranoic. The Commander of the German battleship *Deutschland* had been refused entry to a reception by a junior security man because the Commander didn't have a written invitation — only a phone call from the Secretary of the US Navy! An ambassador recognised him and got him in the side door.

WNBC TV interviewed us and Danny came down to New York, but couldn't find us, so went back to Boston. The rest of us flew back home to Ireland, in the rain!

Three weeks later we six met in Liverpool to bring the boat to Dublin. It was good to be aboard again as a full crew setting sail down the Mersey. The passage across by north Wales was without incident.

8 a.m. the following morning found us off the Kish bank with time on our hands. We weren't due in until 5 p.m. We drifted and fished, catching the makings of lunch. We toasted our 'Bád Mór' with bourbon and sailed into Dun Laoghaire — and later to her moorings on the Liffey.

Ar ais arís.

Would you do it again?

Certainly, once. Not a repeat, of course. To be the crew of the first Galway Hooker to sail to America is something we will always savour. There is nothing unique in sailing the Atlantic in a small boat, but for the most part they are yachts, built as pleasure vehicles. To take a native Irish sailing boat, which had already seen a half century of hard daily service off our west coast, across to America under sail, that was the essential satisfaction.

Much is made of the weatherly qualities of the Hooker and similar old working sailing vessels. This is true in comparison with the average coasting yacht, but to say they could sail any-

143

Our friends sailed with us in New York harbour.

4 July is Independence Day in America!

where is not true. We took the easiest route we could across the Atlantic and we were still put to severe test on several occasions. That she responded is due in part to a measure of luck. Her long bowsprit, her internal ballast and her unwieldy gaff are inherently vulnerable in severe ocean weather conditions. Other aspects such as her heavy-weather helm, the weight of her rig and running gear are potentially dangerous in so far as they can quickly tire the crew in handling them.

Could you have done it without laying-up in the Canary Islands?

Without a doubt we could have sailed across without calling in there, not to mind laying up the boat there. However, it did reduce the time to be taken off work in 1986, for most of the lads. In hindsight, the time-saving was less than expected and the travelling, storage and work required on the boat in the Canaries cost a lot of money. If we were doing the voyage again we would not lay up, but would do it in one season.

However, the compensations were ample. We have experienced peoples and places throughout the southern part of the North Atlantic that one never would if one were going by the most direct practicable route.

Did you have any health problems?

Thanks be to God, none at all. Our medical kit, containing morphine, syringes, dental equipment and so on, was untouched. There may have been a shortage of the less exotic first-aid stuff, such as Elastoplast and headache tablets.

How were your communications?

Adequate in so far as they were called on. Our shortwave Ham set-up was successful. However, were we doing the voyage or a similar one again I would like to have an all-band transceiver so that the commercial marine bands too, would have been available to us; particularly those in the medium frequency range for weather forecasts.

How did your food work out?

Grand, in general. But fresh food went off quicker than we expected. Our staples of potatoes, rice and bread mix were fine, and lasted well. Spices and garnishes were important to make

We re-rigged in Liverpool.

It was very good to be back!

them attractive. Long-life milk transforms voyaging; I like my tea and coffee with milk and various white powders are not a substitute.

Don't depend on fish. When caught consider them as a treat.

Is it worth going so far south to catch the trade winds?

I'll never know for sure. Our total 'sea time' was sixteen days to Tenerife, twenty-six to Bermuda and six to the States, that's forty-eight days in all for 5,500 miles. I don't think we would have beaten that by attempting the direct 3,000 mile route with its prevailing head winds and contrary current. The intermediate 'Azores' route would probably have taken about the same time but the sailing would not have been as good.

How did you afford all this? How did you get off work?

If we had waited until we could afford it we never would have left. We borrowed, on the expectation of getting financial support or sponsorship, but that never happened on the scale we had hoped. With help from our friends, proceeds of dances, equipment from well-disposed firms, the selling of tee-shirts, brochures and plaques in the States, we managed to keep going. We still have what Kevin describes as 'some financial loose ends'.

Our time off work was unpaid leave of absence, combined with annual holidays.

How did you get on together? Were there any rows?

Because of the way we came together, as friends from way back mostly, we got on very well. In a voyage or an expedition, personality clashes are much more likely to occur than in a race situation, where the singleminded objective of going as fast as possible is paramount.

We would in retrospect lay a lot of emphasis on all round personality and general ability rather than on 'hot-shot' sailing capacity. We had no serious rows and any differences of opinion were invariably when a choice appeared possible in shore arrangements. Of course experience at sea was necessary, as was an ability to put up with a certain amount of hardship. You do not grow soft on the *Saint Patrick*.

What have you planned next?

We can truthfully say, nothing at all, notwithstanding that the Mayor of Newport wants us to come over for the 500th anniversary of Columbus's discovery of America — in 1992. We are now returned to the mainstream of normal living again, at our work and with our families.

We have been to the mountain! We are glad to be back.

Acknowledgements

Eugene Magee Travel for very generous assistance. Kevin Kelly Interiors. Liam Barry. Paddy Norris. Maureen Barry. Gerry Casey, Industrial Print Ltd, for commemorative plaques. Tony Lord, Celtic glass, for commemorative glasses. Peter White, for tee-shirts and radio. Donegal Woollen Products for sweaters. Bunkside reading from Brandon, Blackstaff, Stanford, Mercier, Ward River, Conway, O'Brien, Gill & Macmillan and Wolfhound. Simpson Laurence for anchor. C. J. Haughey. Mike Dennehy. Brian Quinn. Erin Foods, for dried food. J. Lyons & Co. for tea. Bewley's Cafes Ltd. for coffee. Gendist for fire extinguishers. Gael-Linn for cassettes. Munster Simms Hardware, for a pressure cooker. B.P. Ireland for diesel. Turmec Engineering, Rathcarn. Chloride (Ireland) for batteries. Calor Kosangas for bottled gas. Harrington & Goodlass Wall for paint. Alfred Bird & Sons (Ireland) Ltd. Maxwell House. Irish Biscuits Ltd. Coca-Cola Bottling Co. Munster Simms, Belfast for Whale pump. Lynch Reinhardt. Kodak (Ireland) Ltd. for film. Ever Ready (Ireland) Ltd. for flash lamp batteries. Sile De Barra, for sterling work over a long period, a special thank you. Jerry Egan and Tom Madden, New York Shipping Agents. Eamon & Clare Doran, New York. Jack Donohue, New York. Michael Glynn, New York. Larry and Jeanne Ottway, New York. Carmel & Joe Cralle, New York. Garnett & Keegans for fishing equipment. Donal Skehan. Agfa Gevaert Ltd for film. Maura O Mealoid, Boston. Anne & Ray Reilly, Boston. Ann Dougherty, Boston. John Curran, Boston. Ann Graham, Boston. John Joyce, Boston. Brigid & Colm Riordan, Boston. Savin Hill Y.C., Boston. Fred Barry. F. Barrett & Co. Ltd., for film. Mike Mulcahy, 'CPJ', Boston. Gertrude & Cecil Downs, Bermuda. Helen &

Tom Gallagher, Bermuda. Elizabeth Jones, Bermuda. Jean & Joe Wakefield, Bermuda. Brenda & Barry Meade, Bermuda. Denise & John Kane, Bermuda. Murteen Bawn Breathnach, Cashla. Cumann Drámaoíochta, Rathcarn. Comharcumann Rathcarn. Mayor Pat Kirby, Newport, Rhode Island. Pat Horgan, Christies, Newport. Jerry Cahill, 'EI 6BT' and the 'group'. Dr David Thomas for medical advice. Dermot O'Sullivan for dental advice. B. Daly (Ireland) Ltd., for Irish Mist. Con McCann, Connacht. Udaras Na Gaeltachta. Hickey Brothers, London. Goodalls, Eugene Greene. Dr John Madden. Austin Duke. Hygea, John Coyle. Gillette, Sean Mallin. Roma Foods. Curran Photographers. Paraic MacDonagh. Clem Kelly. Pat Ardagh for emergency food. Leo Ganter. John Kelly. Joe Murphy. Tom Roche and Paraic MacLoughlin. Pete Hogan and Andrew O'Hanlon.

Michael Gill for his enthusiastic guidance in turning a story into a book.

Louis Purton and Liam Canavan whose help in preparing the boat was invaluable.

To all of our friends and well wishers on both sides of the Atlantic who supported the fund raising events.

Preparations

The Galway Hooker is a boat decked only to the mast. Aft of that, where her cargo went, she is open. *Saint Patrick* had been cruising for some years. Modifications to make this possible had previously been carried out. She already had a Perkins 4.236 engine and was decked.

For the Atlantic voyage the following changes were made: Cockpit reduced in size and partially sealed. It was not made self-draining. Trim Tab fitted to rudder. Shaft brake installed. Oven installed. Additional fixing bolts to cabin top. Floor boards bolted down to retain ballast. Additional ballast installed internally. No changes were made to the Rigging or Sails.

The following equipment was taken on, additional to that previously installed: Sommerkamp FT-7B. Short wave transceiver, Long Wire Antenna. EPIRB Distress Beacon. 8-Man Liferaft (in lieu of 4-man). Dan Buoy & Strobe Light. 60lb CQR Anchor + Hurricane ground chain. Two Fire Extinguishers. 120 amp. hr. battery for Radio use. Whale 25 Pump. Two Buckets. Kelvin Hughes Sextant, Quartz watch, Astronomical Tables. Charts and Sailing Directions. Three flash lamps. Spare batteries and bulbs.

The Stores List for the crossing was based on a 6 man crew and a probable passage time of 30 days. A contingency of 50% extra was provided for. Sealed emergency Liferaft Stores were carried in addition, intended to provide minimal sustenance for 3 weeks.

Water usage was based on $\frac{1}{2}$-gallon per man/day.

151

The following was the list:

Water, 115 gallons
Diesel, 80 gallons
Potatoes, three four-stone bags
Bread Mix
Rice, 18 lbs
Oranges, 15 dozen
Grapefruit, 6 doz
Eggs, 10 doz
Margarine, 14 lbs
Jam, 15 lbs
Tea, 24 doz. bags
Long Life Milk, 24 litres
Sugar, 8 lbs
Soups, 200 Hot Cup
Cheese, 4 lb
Pickles, 2 jars
Onions, 4 stone
Carrots, 4 stone
Ground Coffee
Instant Coffee
Tinned Tuna
Tinned Ham
Garlic, String
Pasta, 6x1 lb. packets
Salt, 3 lbs
Tinned sweetcorn, 12 tins

Corn Oil, ½ gallon
Vinegar
Tomatoes (green), 24 dozen
Bananas (green)
Apples
Melons
Tinned Peas
Tinned Tomatoes
Tinned Beans
Peppers, red & green
Ground pepper & spices
Curry powder
Ploughmans Pickle
Mars Bars, 3 Boxes
Erin Dried Dinners
Erin Little Dinners
Erin Vegetables
Emergency Liferaft Rations
Figs, 20 Kg
Bars of glucose, nut,
    almond 20 kg

Wine, 12 cases
Spirits, 10 bottles
Soft Drinks, 6 doz
Soft Drink Powder, 24 Packets

Food — a note by Johnny Walsh

Everyone loved the breakfast. You'd nearly want to clip our wings after the amount of eggs we ate in the first three weeks or so. They formed the basis of practically every breakfast and were cooked in just about every way imaginable. Generally, each pair on watch would alternate cooking each other's breakfast and there was always something extra nice in having it handed to you while sailing in the cool of morning. Also included was any combination of toast, fried bread, tomatoes, beans or whatever happened to be open or handy. Washed down with a mug of tea or coffee, this would set you up for the day. Of course this careful and loving preparation had to be carried out in silence as the slightest clang of a pot could wake four hungry men who would all then want breakfast in bed.

The rest of the day consisted of snacks, lunch, dinner and tot. Snacks were mainly of fruit with the odd Mars Bar. Later in the passage tastes matured as the aroma of freshly baking currant cake and brown bread filled the cabin.

The three watch pairs rotated cooking on a daily basis, taking charge of lunch, evening meal and all the wash-up. As might be expected, standards varied from the sublime to the ridiculous but overall the quality was good. The lunch ingredients were usually rice, onions and mayonnaise backed up by moderate portions of ham or tuna. A variety of other items were then added either for taste, presentation or convenience.

In the heat of the afternoon most liquids were drunk. The staple was Birds 'Apeel' in quart sachets.

While lunches were often taken by all the crew on deck it was normal for most to sit below for dinner, with one on the helm and sometimes another for company.

For dinner the base was usually potato or curry. We ate a large amount of onions which were always popular. Other than the odd fish caught, we were restricted to tinned ham, tinned tuna and dried foods such as chicken stew and goulash.

With the evening meal we would have wine from our 'cellar'. Officially we were restricted to two 75cl. bottles of Rioja per day between six. Occasionally, of course, the 'one at lunch and one at dinner' became one and two, but with no ill-effect. Part of the reason for this was the amount of spillage due to rolling of the boat. The day finished with a tot of spirits.

In bad weather none of the above applied, with no wine or spirits. You ate what you could, when you could.

Insurances

The vessel's normal Marine Policy was extended to cover the Atlantic voyage and United States Coastal Waters for an additional premium of £250. To insure against the possibility of very high medical costs while in the Bermuda/United States area a 'travel' policy was taken out on the crew. 'Power of Attorney' was prepared and arranged on an individual basis so that the crew's domestic financial affairs might, if necessary, be dealt with. A less likely but potentially more serious aspect of this is that in the event of anyone being drowned, and the body not recovered, their financial assets are frozen for seven years. The Power of Attorney gets over this.

Medical Stores
In addition to normal first aid material we took the following prescribed drugs and medicines. A Doctor's Letter of Authority and the Chemist's Invoice for these was carried.

Morphine, 10 Ampoules, 10 mgs for severe pain, emergency only.
Pethidine, 20 tablets, 50 mgs for severe pain, emergency only.
Doloxene Co, 100 tablets for severe pain.
Lomotil, 100 tablets for diarrhoea.
Hostacyclene, 100 tablets, 250 mg. A broad spectrum antibiotic.
Chloromycetin ointment, for eye infections.
Maxolon, 100 tablets for vomiting.
Betnovate Cream for allergic rashes.

Summary accounts by Kevin Cronin

EXPENDITURE	£	£
Equipment		
New Life Raft (trade-in)	321	
Oven, Distress Beacon, Danboy Strobe light	445	
Shortwave Radio	550	
First Aid	42	
Flares	68	
Miscellaneous	53	1,479
Improvements/Repairs to Boat		
Materials	509	
Shipwright	230	
Repairs — Canaries	1,562	2,301
Fund Raising Costs		
Postage, Stationery, Telephone, Carriage	557	
Receptions and Entertainment	410	
Plaques, photos	567	
Brochures	300	1,834
Insurance — Boat		1,267
— Personal		380
Camera & Film		177
Boatyard costs — Canaries		1,197
Living expenses Canaries/Bermuda/USA		2,503
Food for boat (mostly donated)		467

Fares Canaries-Dublin/Dublin-Canaries/		
New York-Dublin		3,710
Boat freight New York — Liverpool		4,500
Miscellaneous		145
		19,960

INCOME	£	£
P. J. Carroll (Freight costs — boat home)	5,200	
Other Donations	2,381	

Fund raising activities

● Dance Blackrock RFC	2,708	
● Dance Boston	1,420	
● Receptions Boston	1,586	
● Sale of Tee-Shirts, plaques & boat trips		
in New York	2,812	16,107
Deficit (financed personally by crew)		3,853

The above deficit does not include loss of pay of crew for unpaid leave of absence from work of £7,000 approx.